Analytical Models
for Urban
and Regional Planning

Analytical Models for Urban and Regional Planning

IAN MASSER

Halsted Press Division
John Wiley & Sons, Inc
New York

ISBN 0 470-58025-9
Library of Congress Catalog Card Number 72-3447

Set in 10 on 12 point Times
and printed in Great Britain
by Bell and Bain Ltd Glasgow
and published in the United States
by Halsted Press Division
John Wiley & Sons, Inc,
New York

Contents

1. Introduction

One of the most serious problems facing urban and regional planning at the present time is the difficulty of relating anticipated needs to past experience. Looking ahead, many experts foresee an increasing pace of social change which will create new tasks that challenge the traditional expertise of urban and regional planners. In the face of this challenge past experience provides an unsatisfactory basis for future action. If anything it appears to be backward looking in terms of its achievements rather than forward looking. The concept of the new town, for instance, must be viewed essentially as a solution to the congestion of nineteenth-century cities rather than twentieth-century metropolitan sprawl.

The realisation of this dilemma has stimulated a radical review of large parts of the field of urban and regional planning. Gradually, it is becoming accepted that future planning will be much more tentative than planning even in the recent past, and also that much greater emphasis will be placed on the analysis and understanding of the basic processes of social change than before. Urban and regional planners have been forced to look elsewhere for guidance as to the methods that they should adopt in future work, and they have been strongly influenced by developments since the war in respect of systems analysis, cybernetics, operations research, and related fields which have culminated in the spectacular technological achievements in space.

These developments contain two important messages for urban and regional planners. Firstly, the success of the aerospace projects in particular, has shown them that complex systems can be successfully controlled, and the apparent analogy between these systems and urban and regional systems has encouraged many planners to redefine their role in these terms. Secondly, the analytical methods developed by these disciplines show how complex sets of inter-relationships can be simulated by the use of computer based mathematical models which can also be used as a means of describing the workings of these systems and exploring the consequences of alternative actions. In this way they indicate how urban and regional planners might improve their understanding of social processes and make more informed recommendations to their political masters.

During the last twenty years large parts of urban and regional planning have been transformed by what has come to be called the systems approach and its analytical methods. The first field to be affected by this new approach was the field of transport engineering. Studies carried out in the early fifties such as the Chicago Area Transportation Study, showed that, if a future land use pattern could be defined, a traffic pattern could be predicted which would provide the basis for examining alternative proposals for transportation systems. The techniques developed for these and other contemporary studies had fundamental consequences. According to McLoughlin,

> For the engineering profession these new techniques represented a profound change in outlook. Traditionally approaching their problems as one of the *design of physical equipment* to satisfy functional and cost criteria the engineers were increasingly forced into studies of *human behaviour and choice* in the making of trips and the use of different modes of travel. . . . (McLoughlin, 1969, p. 66)

During the fifties these techniques became increasingly used in transportation planning in North America and tentative attempts were made to develop similar methods in land use planning. By May 1959, experience in transportation planning and land use studies had already reached the state at which it merited a special issue of the *Journal of the American Institute of Planners* entitled 'Land use and traffic models—a progress report'. In a preface to this issue the *Journal*'s editor Melvin Webber highlighted the implications of these behavioural studies for urban and regional planning,

... as we learn more about the constraining consistencies of urban form and function—and then perhaps about the underlying processes for these consistencies—we shall be better able to identify the real range of future choice. If we can understand the limitations upon public choice, we can better identify the real opportunities for deliberately influencing the forms of our future cities. And, as we narrow the margins of uncertainty, we can make more responsible recommendations to the political decision makers whom we serve. (Webber, 1959, p. 55)

After 1960 the range of applications of model building and systems-based studies in planning steadily increased. In May 1965 a further issue of the *Journal of the American Institute of Planners* was devoted to 'Urban development models—new tools for planning'. The range of contributions in this issue extended from transportation and land use studies to housing market analyses and retail location models. It also showed a growing concern for the theoretical and methodological aspects of these new techniques which was largely absent from the earlier volume.

Since 1965 there has been a systematic examination of the whole process of planning. The increased use of operations research methods and goal-oriented techniques in corporate planning by public agencies has compelled urban and regional planners to evaluate their proposals in terms of explicitly stated goals and objectives. In the process a similar transformation in outlook has occurred among urban and regional planners to that experienced by transport engineers in the fifties, and a new methodology of planning is emerging in books such as McLoughlin's *Urban and regional planning—a systems approach* (1969) and Chadwick's *A systems view of planning* (1971).

These changes have not taken place without opposition. Critics of systems planning have scoffed at the tentativeness and apparent uncertainty of many current plans and contrasted them with the vigour and self-assurance of earlier efforts. They have also complained that the use of analytical models to evaluate alternative proposals results in the elimination of visionary and radical schemes and their replacement by mere extrapolations of existing trends. Above all, they have complained that planning is being invaded by an alien methodology with its own esoteric jargon which has little, if any, relevance to the traditional tasks of urban and regional planning.

Some of these criticisms are justified in the light of examples of naïve enthusiasm and the misuse of mathematical techniques in various types of planning situation, but most must be viewed essentially in the context of the basic conflict between the anticipated challenges to future planning and the relevance of past experience. As might be expected, the influence of these methods has been most profound in those parts of the subject which were relatively underdeveloped two decades ago, that is in large-scale strategic planning at the subregional and regional scales, and in population and economic studies where similar developments of systems-based methods have taken place outside the immediate field of planning, and in spatial studies of land use and transportation systems. Conversely, they have had least impact in those parts of the field that were relatively well developed in terms of expertise two decades ago, that is small-scale studies, land use planning, and urban design.

Many of the criticisms also show a fundamental lack of understanding of the new methods which is particularly disturbing because the work of virtually all urban and regional planners is affected in some way by the results of systems-based studies. They are not only a central part of planning activities at the subregional and regional scales but also provide basic briefs for detailed design studies and guidelines for decision taking at the local level. As there is often a distinction between the users of these results and the analysts who produce them it is important that planners whose work involves the interpretation of these findings understand the basic assumptions upon which they are based, and the main principles underlying the methods that are used to produce them. Given this, the development of mathematical models and systems-based methods by competent analysts should enable urban and regional planners to develop a better understanding of the problems that they face which will allow them to formulate more realistic policies and make recommendations with a greater knowledge of their implications than was previously possible.

The aim of this book is to provide an introduction for two kinds of reader to the analytical models that have been developed in respect of three crucial areas of urban and regional planning. First, it is directed towards planners who seek to improve their understanding of methods so that they will be in a better position to evaluate the findings of these studies. Second, it is also intended for those who may be contemplating taking an active part in the future development of analytical models in the planning field or in related disciplines such as geography, economics, sociology, or urban studies.

The three crucial areas are those areas other than transport planning in which analytical models are most frequently used in urban and regional planning at the present time. They are the analysis of population growth, the assessment of the prospects for economic activity, and the spatial organisation of population and economic activity in regions and urban areas. The analytical models that have been developed for transport planning are largely excluded from this introduction on the grounds that they have been dealt with in other works (eg, Bruton (1970) and Creighton (1970)).

The organisation of this book is illustrated in Fig. 1. This shows that the basic elements of population and economic activity and the analytical models are described in overall terms in Chapters 2 and 3, and then in spatial terms in Chapter 4. The distinction between overall studies of population and economic activity and their spatial organisation is an important one from the point of view of planning applications. The ability to evaluate the consequences of possible courses of population growth in terms of the size of the labour force or the number of school-children in the population must be regarded as basic to any planning exercise, and day-to-day decisions must be taken at all levels of planning in relation to certain assumptions that have been made, implicitly or explicitly, about future levels of the population as a whole. Similarly, the overall economic vitality of an urban area or region will have important implications in terms of personal incomes and standards of living that will be reflected in a wide range of planning actions.

The spatial organisation of population and economic activity will affect planning decisions in a different way to the overall studies discussed above. Spatial models will be largely concerned with the factors underlying the distribution of different social groups and

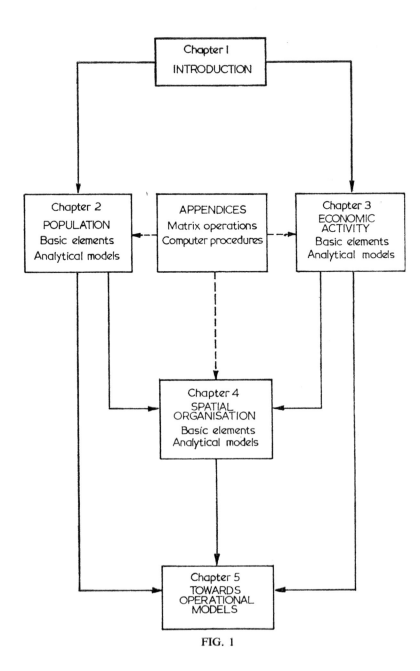

FIG. 1

economic activities within a region or urban area and the ways in which these are reflected in the mixture of activities at various locations in the area under consideration. They will also be concerned with flows of people from home to work or play, and flows of goods between factories not only in terms of their implications for transport studies but also their consequences on patterns of location.

Each of these sections describes the basic elements involved and the analytical models that are available for planning studies. A practical rather than a theoretical approach has been adopted towards the presentation of analytical models which assumes a minimum of mathematical knowledge on the part of the reader. For this reason an introduction to the techniques used in matrix algebra is included in a special appendix for those who are not familiar with this subject.

Some of the basic principles underlying the development of operational models are discussed in the last section, but no attempt has been made to review the improvements and detailed modifications that have been made to analytical models in various operational situations as this lies beyond the scope of an introductory book on the subject. Nor are the data requirements implied by these methods discussed in anything more than general terms, as the nature of possible sources and the use that can be made of them varies considerably in each operational situation.

Mention should also be made of two special features of the presentation of this material. In view of the wide range of literature that has been covered by the book and the difficulties experienced by an introductory reader when faced with a long list of references, the conventional bibliography has been augmented by a short section at the end of each chapter which discusses the references in terms of possible areas for further study. Secondly, a special appendix containing basic computer procedures for the methods described in the text is included so that simple examples can be worked out mechanically by readers with access to a computer. In this way readers can avoid the bulk of the repetitious calculations involved in even some simple worked examples and have the opportunity to further deepen their understanding of the basic methods by inventing fresh problems and evaluating their results.

Terminology

Given this approach, the only matter that must be cleared up before the start of the next chapter is terminology. The term 'model' in particular needs clarification. A mathematical model of the kind described in this book is, like a child's doll or an architect's model of a building, a purposeful abstraction from complex reality. The process of model development is one by which those features of the subject under consideration that are essential to the purpose of the task are identified and incorporated in the model while unnecessary details are eliminated. In the case of urban and regional systems, however, the identification of what is essential or not essential must also relate to the development and verification of theories about these systems. The kind of model that is discussed in subsequent sections, then, is not only an abstraction or simplification of reality, but it is, according to Britton Harris 'an experimental design based on a theory' (Harris 1966, p. 265) which involves in Lowry's terms 'the application of theories to a concrete case' (Lowry 1965, p. 160).

A mathematical model is one in which the inter-relationships between different elements of the system that is under consideration are expressed as a series of equations. These equations contain two types of variable. The term 'exogenous' is usually used to refer to variables whose numerical values are determined outside the model, whereas the term 'endogenous' is usually used to refer to variables whose numerical values are determined by the model. The estimation of the values of the endogenous variables can be seen as the basic problem of modelling but the quality of the results will be dependent on the extent to which two different sets of criteria are met by the model. They will be dependent firstly on the assumptions that are implicitly made in the specification of the exogenous variables and secondly, on the ways in which the inter-relationships that are contained within the model have been specified.

The mathematical models that are described in subsequent chapters are essentially predictive models, in the sense that they are used to predict values which can be compared with observations from other sources. As a result, a predictive model is not necessarily a forecasting model as it can be used to estimate the distribution of activities at one point in time as well as to estimate future states of these activities. Prediction is a fundamental part of the process of testing an operational model when the values that have been predicted by the model are compared with those observed in reality. This process, which is usually termed calibration, is in effect an evaluation of the results produced by the model, not in terms of their usefulness for decision making, but in terms of the extent to which the theories represented by the model can be shown to represent real situations.

In addition to these terms a number of other specialist terms will be explained in relation to particular models. A general explanation of the most commonly used terms can be found in Britton Harris' paper 'Urban development models—a gloss on lacklustre terms' (Harris 1965).

Further Reading

A great deal has been written about the problems facing urban and regional planning and the relevance of a systems-based approach to the subject. The best way of getting the flavour of this debate is by examining some recent volumes of the professional journals such as the *Journal of the American Institute of Planners* and the *Journal of the Royal Town Planning Institute,* but a classic statement of the problems facing planning in an environment of change can be found in two papers by Webber (1968 and 1969) while Bolan's (1967) discussion of emerging views in planning is a useful summary of the different kinds of stance that have been adopted by practitioners in recent years. The development of the systems approach in planning is described in general terms by McLoughlin in his book (McLoughlin, 1969, pp. 58–74), and by the same author at greater length in a review article which also contains an extensive bibliography (McLoughlin and Webster, 1970).

The use of analytical models in planning is discussed in an early paper by Harris (1960). Some of the ideas put forward in this paper are further developed in relation to the whole field of metropolitan policy making in a later paper by the same author (Harris, 1968a) and also in a review article by Wilson (1968) which lists most of the basic references in the field. The field of models in general is described in a straight-forward way by Loewenstein (1966), while Lowry's short course in model design (Lowry, 1965) provides an essential introduction to the principles of operational modelling for urban and regional planners.

2. Population

This section discusses the problems involved and the techniques that are available to urban and regional planners for the analysis and projection of population change. The results of these studies are of vital importance to this kind of planning as the scale of population growth affects land requirements for housing and many other urban activities, and influences many of the key investment decisions that have to be made by both public and private agencies. In the public sector population growth will be a major factor in decisions about investment in schools and hospitals, roads and public transport, together with the development of public utilities such as electricity and water supply. In the private sector population growth prospects will be felt in a wide variety of ways. For instance, the level of production in industries serving local markets is likely to be closely related to growth. In another case, growth will be reflected in the size of the local labour force which may be an important factor in plans for the expansion of production.

Generally it will be necessary to consider the structural composition of the population as well as the aggregate growth of an area treated as a whole. Obviously many activities are restricted to certain age groups and/or certain types of population, and an analysis of school requirements or provision for old people need take account of only a segment of the total population. Similar conditions are also likely to apply to projections of the labour force or household formation but in these cases

B

it will be necessary to examine population growth in terms of marital status as well as age composition.

For some studies an assessment must be made of the relative status of population change in one area as against other areas. At the purely local level this question is best treated as an allocation or distribution problem within the context of the area as a whole. It will be discussed as such later in this book (Chapter 4). However, at a subregional level an analysis of this kind will indicate the competitive position of the area under consideration in relation to the country as a whole.

The models of population that have been developed for planning purposes reflect these requirements. Generally they are predictive models which are capable of disaggregation wherever appropriate in terms of age, sex, and marital status. And as a result of recent work, they can be formulated in such a way that they can be extended to examine the area under consideration in relation to other areas.

This chapter is divided into two main parts dealing respectively with the definition of the elements of population change, and the techniques used in the analytical process. The distinction between elements and techniques has been made deliberately so that important concepts such as fertility and migration can be discussed separately from the methods used to handle them in the analytical models.

Basic Elements

There are three main components of population change. These measure respectively, the increase in population arising as a result of births during the period under consideration, the decrease in population due to deaths during this period, and the extent to which the population at the start of the period has subsequently been affected by the movement of people into and out of the area under consideration. This process may be summarised as follows

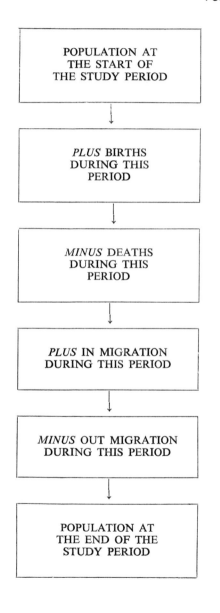

1 *Births*

Births are normally considered in relation to some measure of potential fertility such as the number of women in the child-bearing age group. In table 2.1, for example, births are expressed in terms of the

TABLE 2.1

Live births per 1000 women in England and Wales by age of mother at birth

Age of Mother at Birth	Live births per 1000 women during			
	1953	1958	1963	1968
15–19	22·03	31·04	40·02	48·80
20–24	134·60	158·30	178·96	160·87
25–29	139·53	161·41	183·84	160·42
30–34	89·03	93·62	105·64	87·87
35–39	44·23	45·76	48·36	40·24
40–44	12·96	12·00	13·42	10·45
15–44*	73·73	83·69	95·04	84·78

Source: Registrar General's Statistical Review for England and Wales. Part II Population Tables. 1953, 1958, 1963, 1968.
* Assuming 1000 in each age group.

number of live births per 1000 women of each age category during the years under review. For projection purposes these measures must be converted into fertility rates which indicate the probability of a woman who falls into one of these age categories giving birth over a given period of time. In the table, the fertility rate can be calculated by dividing each figure by 1000. In this way the probability of a woman aged between 15 and 19 giving birth during 1953 would be 0·02203, or 0·13460 for a woman aged between 20 and 24 in the same year.

The table also shows that fertility rates are highly sensitive indices which can fluctuate considerably during the time span involved in most of the population projections that might be made for planning purposes. Consequently they are a major source of error in these projections, not only because of the difficulties involved in anticipating the scale and direction of these fluctuations but also because any errors in estimate become cumulative during the later years of the projection when babies 'born' in the initial years have aged sufficiently to be in a position to produce their own babies.

These problems can be illustrated by comparing the fertility rates for the best year in table 2.1 (1963) with those for the worst year (1953). If a constant population of 1000 is assumed for each of the child-bearing age groups, it will be seen that the number of live births per 1000 women in 1963 was 95·04 as against only 73·73 in 1953. A projection based on 1963 figures would produce 29 per cent more babies than one based on 1953 figures. If this difference was allowed to continue until the babies 'born' in the projection had aged sufficiently to produce their own families, the number of second-generation births estimated on the basis of the 1963 figures would be over 66 per cent greater than that estimated from the 1953 figures (ie, $(129/100) \times (129/100)$).

No analysis of births in any depth can take place without a parallel study of marriages because the vast majority of births are legitimate. Marriage rates are likely to influence the number of births in two main ways. Firstly, there are likely to be variations in space as well as time in the proportion of married people in a population. Spatial variations may be of considerable importance in certain cases. For instance, the process of selection for new and expanding towns tends to favour married couples at the expense of single people in the child-bearing age groups. As a result the probability of giving birth is likely to be considerably higher than the general average for these age groups, particularly during the early years of the development. In a completely different situation, the presence of large numbers of young and single women in the inner areas of large cities such as London may give rise to fertility rates which are noticeably lower than the general average. Secondly, the duration of the marriage is likely to affect the number of potential births in that the probability of giving birth declines progressively as the length of marriage increases. If the average age at marriage goes down, the fertility of the older age groups will decline, and, conversely, if the average age at marriage increases, the fertility of these groups will increase.

As well as variations in the proportions of married people in the population and the duration of the marriage, the number of births may also reflect variations in attitudes towards family building and birth control which are an expression of differences in social class, race, and religion. Generally, it has been found that fertility rates correlate negatively with social class, and also that they are higher in coloured groups and Roman Catholic populations than for white groups or Protestants, but statements of this kind have no universal validity. For example, a comparison of international differences would show that Catholicism is as 'responsible' for the low fertility rates of Italy as the high ones in Ireland.

2 Deaths

Death tends to be treated in population studies as a negative element in that the analyst is mainly interested in those people who survive to form part of the population at a given point in time rather than those who have been prevented from reaching this state by death. Consequently it is measured in terms of the chances of survival rather than the chances of dying. The likelihood of survival is expressed in the form of a life table which indicates the number of people out of a given number of births who would survive until each age category if they were subject to the recorded death rates of the period. In table 2.2 the number of men and women surviving is expressed in terms of a standard 10 000 births. It shows that 3963 out of 10 000 men and 6147 out of 10 000 women would reach the age of 75 on the basis of the death rates recorded for 1968. For analytical purposes, these chances can be expressed in the form of the survival rate which indicates the probability that a person in one age group will survive to reach another age group. In the table the chances of a boy at birth reaching the age of 75 would be 3963/10 000, that is, 0·3963, on the basis of 1968 rates. Similar

TABLE 2.2

Abridged Life Tables for England and Wales 1958, 1963, and 1968

| | Survivors per 10 000 births subject to recorded death rates of period | | | | | |
| | Males | | | Females | | |
Age	1958	1963	1968	1958	1963	1968
0	10 000	10 000	10 000	10 000	10 000	10 000
15	9666	9682	9718	9746	9756	9785
30	9523	9539	9588	9671	9688	9722
45	9233	9252	9320	9452	9476	9527
60	7855	7886	8008	8664	8694	8768
75	3888	3803	3963	5882	5912	6147

Source: Registrar General's Statistical Review for England and Wales.
Part I Medical Tables, 1958, 1963.
Part II Population Tables 1968.

probabilities can also be derived from this table for intervening age groups. For instance, the probability that a man aged 60 will survive until the age of 75 would be 3963/8008, that is 0·4949, on the basis of 1968 rates.

In contrast to fertility rates survival rates vary only slightly over the time span involved in most planning exercises. For this reason, and also because errors in estimating the number of deaths do not have the cumulative effects that are associated with births, they constitute a relatively stable element in this kind of study. In the table, for example, the largest difference between the survival rates occurs in respect of the number of women reaching 75, but even in this case, the highest estimate (1968) is only five per cent more than the lowest estimate (1958).

In spite of their relative stability over time survival rates may vary quite considerably between areas. Like births, these variations may reflect differences in social class in that there is generally a negative correlation between death rates and social class. In the case of deaths, they are also likely to be related to the proportion of the population engaged in relatively dangerous jobs such as mining or the armed forces.

3 *Migration*

The act of migration cannot be defined in the relatively precise terms that are associated with the acts of birth and death. Because of this, it presents problems of definition and measurement which are not found in respect of the other elements of population change. To obtain the estimates given in table 2.3, for example, the act of migration is defined as 'anyone whose usual address on census date (23 April 1961) was different from their usual address on 23 April 1960'.

This definition, however, is only partial as it excludes, for instance, short-term moves during the year in question. As long as an individual was residing at the same address on the two specified dates he would not be classified as a migrant, irrespective of where he might have been living during the period. Similarly it ignores multiple moves. In this table, a distinction is made only between migrants and non-migrants, and not between the number of moves made by migrants.

It should also be noted that the accounting system used for recording migration in table 2.3 is not comprehensive. There is a basic difference between immigrants and emigrants, in that an immigrant in table 2.3 is someone resident at an address in 1961 who was not there in 1960 irrespective of his place of origin. An emigrant in this table, on the other

TABLE 2.3

Migration in England and Wales 1960–61

	Migrants within area	*Migrants per 1000 residents*		
		Immigrants	*Emigrants**	*Migration balance**
England and Wales	98	7	*	*
within a local authority area	51			
between local authority areas	47			
Conurbations	81	20	20	0
Areas outside conurbations:				
Urban areas with populations of 100 000 or more	69	32	33	−1
Urban areas with populations between 50 000 and 100 000	64	49	40	9
Urban areas with populations of less than 50 000	64	42	33	9
Rural districts	57	54	30	24

Source: Table 4 Migration Tables. 1961 Census

* Persons leaving England and Wales not recorded

hand, is someone who has moved only to another address within England and Wales, and persons leaving the country have not been recorded.

Population change analyses are not concerned with migration in itself but migration across the boundaries of the area under consideration. When migration is redefined in this way it becomes purely relative. In table 2.3 some 98 out of every 1000 people changed addresses during the year in question. None of these would be classified as migrants in an analysis of population changes in the country as a whole. But nearly half of these people (47/1000) crossed a local authority boundary during their move, and would require consideration in the migration component of local authority population change analysis.

Two different measures can be used in the analysis of migration. Firstly, there is the net change, which measures the extent to which the population of an area will change during a given period as a result of migration. The net change or migration balance can be calculated for an area by subtracting the number of emigrants from the number of immigrants. In table 2.3, for example, the net change per 1000 population for rural districts is $+24$ whereas that for urban areas with populations of 100 000 or more is -1. In the former case, the effect of migration per person would be $1+24/1000$, that is 1·024, while, in the case of the latter it would be $1-1/1000$, that is 0·999. Secondly, there is gross interaction, which recognizes that every act of migration involves two populations, and considers immigrants and emigrants to the area under consideration also in terms of their respective origins and destinations outside this area. In this case the probability of an individual staying or moving during a given period of time would be calculated in relation to the population of the area of residence at the start of the period. In the case of the conurbations in table 2.3, the probability of emigrating is 20/1000, that is 0·020 while that of staying is $(1000-20)/1000$, that is 0·980.

In view of the difficulties involved in its definition and measurement it is particularly unfortunate that migration is generally the most important of the three components of change in population projections for territorial subdivisions at, and below the subregional level. It is also disturbing to find that migration rates are often liable to fluctuate considerably during the time spans envisaged in most planning studies, and that, like fertility rates, any errors in the estimated rates will have a cumulative effect on the estimates of future population, in that an

TABLE 2.4

Migration flows between Merseyside, the rest of the North West Region and the rest of England and Wales, 1960–61 and 1965–66

		To:							
		Merseyside		Rest of NW Region		Rest of England and Wales		Total	
		60/61	65/66	60/61	65/66	60/61	65/66	60/61	65/66
From:	Merseyside 60/61	—		14 140		13 130		27 270	
	65/66		—		20 600		12 360		32 960
	Rest of NW Region 60/61	7320		—		52 850		60 170	
	65/66		8120		—		56 760		64 880
	Rest of England and Wales 60/61	9200		46 280		—		55 480	
	65/66		10 040		53 770		—		63 810
	Total 60/61	16 520		60 420		65 980		142 920	
	65/66		18 160		74 370		69 120		161 650

Net Balance

	1960/61	1965/6
Merseyside	− 10 750	− 14 800
Rest of North West Region	+ 250	+ 9490
Rest of England and Wales	+10 500	+ 5310

Source: **Census** 1961 and 1966 Migration Tables.

overestimate of emigrants will take potential parents out of the analysis while an underestimate of immigrants will not bring all the potential parents into the analysis.

Some of these problems are illustrated by table 2.4 which shows the migration flows between Merseyside, its regional hinterland and the rest of England and Wales for 1960/61 and 1965/66. It shows that the net balance of migration from Merseyside in 1965/66 was nearly half as much again as that for 1960/61. Consequently any prediction for the later year which was based on the experience of the earlier year would considerably underestimate the effect of migration. Several further problems emerge when these flows are viewed in terms of interaction. Firstly, the total number of migrants in 1965/66 was 13 per cent higher than the total number in 1960/61. Secondly, there are major changes in the volume of movement in some parts of the matrix. The increase in emigration from Merseyside in 1965/66 was entirely due to an increase in flows from Merseyside to its regional hinterland and there was an absolute decline in movement from Merseyside to the rest of England and Wales in this year.

In addition to personal interaction, matrices of this kind of migration must also be viewed in relation to household formation. It is likely to be at its highest at times when households are being created as a result of marriage, and also to a lesser extent, when households break up as a result of the death of one of their members. The probability of migration, or potential mobility, also increases with social class, but it should also be borne in mind that certain kinds of occupations such as the Armed Forces or civil servants, involve a high degree of mobility irrespective of social class.

Analytical Models

Population models are used in planning to analyse and to predict the demographic structure of the population of a given area at certain points in time from a known population on the basis of stated assumptions about the number of births and deaths that will occur during each period and the effects of migration on the area under consideration.

In the following discussion the basic cohort survival method that has been developed for analysing the natural increase of population (ie, the change that is due to births–deaths) is presented first, then this simple model is extended to include net migration. After this, further extensions which enable a more elaborate treatment of interaction between several regions are considered, as are the ways in which the basic model can be disaggregated by sex and marital status. A brief summary of the general principles that should be borne in mind when considering the development of population models concludes this section.

1 *The Basic Cohort Survival Model*

The standard method used for population projection is known as the cohort survival method. It is based on the concept of the cohort, which in a population model, represents a group of people of the same age. If the initial population of one of these age cohorts is known, the number of people in the group who will survive to reach another age group can be estimated by multiplying the initial population by the survival rates for the intervening age groups:

$$p_{n+1}^{(t+1)} = sp_n^{(t)} \tag{2.1}$$

where $p_n^{(t)}$ is the population of age group n at time t

$p_{n+1}^{(t+1)}$ is the population of age group $n+1$ at time $t+1$

s is the probability that a person aged n at time t will survive to reach age $n+1$ at time $t+1$

This may be illustrated by a numerical example using the figures discussed earlier in relation to the life table (table 2.2). Given a cohort of 10 000 baby boys in 1968, and given that the chances of survival for each age group remain the same as in 1968, it can be estimated that 9718 of these will reach the age of 15 in 1983 (ie, 10 000 × 0.9718), 9588 will survive until they are 30 in 1998 (ie, 10 000 × 0·9718 or 9718 × (9588/9718)), and so forth.

In this way the number of survivors for each group can be estimated for a given point in time, and by summing up the estimates for each cohort, the total number of survivors can be calculated from an initial population for a given point in time. A similar method can be used to estimate the number of births over a given time period. This involves multiplying an initial population of a given age group by the fertility of the relevant age group, ie:

$$^{(t)}b_n^{(t+1)} = fp_n^{(t)} \tag{2.2}$$

where $^{(t)}b_n^{(t+1)}$ is the number of births between time t and $t+1$ to mothers aged n at time t

      f is the probability that a person aged n at time t will give birth between time t and time $t+1$

      $p_n^{(t)}$ is the population aged n at time t

By summing the numbers predicted for each cohort of mothers, the total number of births during each projection period can be estimated. These estimates form new cohorts whose survivorship can then be projected, if desired, for later projection periods. In this way a self generating or recursive model of population can be initiated which will estimate the age distribution of the population for any future point in time on the basis of predetermined assumptions about mortality and fertility.

The chances of survival and giving birth can be combined into one operation by formulating this simple model in matrix terms. This procedure not only makes the exercises computationally easier, but also clarifies the mechanism of the projection process and enables a more sophisticated treatment of migration than would normally be possible. It involves the concept of vector and matrix multiplication which is explained for those not familiar with matrix algebra in appendix A.

As a result of the work of Keyfitz (1964) and Rogers (1966, 1968) the cohort survival model can be reformulated as follows. The age distribution of an initial population consisting of n equal age groups at time t can be denoted by an $n \times 1$ column vector $\mathbf{p}^{(t)}$,

$$\mathbf{p}^{(t)}_{n \times 1} = \begin{bmatrix} p_1 \\ p_2 \\ p_3 \\ p_4 \\ \cdot \\ \cdot \\ \cdot \\ \cdot \\ p_n \end{bmatrix}$$

To estimate the number of people in each age group who will survive to the next period at time $t+1$ who will be represented in the $n \times 1$ column vector ($\mathbf{p}^{(t+1)}$), it is necessary to define an $n \times n$ matrix operator $\mathbf{G}$ which can be used to premultiply the initial population vector so that

$$\mathbf{G}\mathbf{p}^{(t)} = \mathbf{p}^{(t+1)} \tag{2.3}$$

The matrix operator $\mathbf{G}$ will contain the probabilities of both births and survival during this period. The survival component of the matrix will be located in the following way:

$$\mathbf{S}_{n \times n} = \begin{bmatrix} 0 & 0 & 0 & 0 & \cdot & \cdot & 0 \\ s_{21} & 0 & 0 & 0 & \cdot & \cdot & 0 \\ 0 & s_{32} & 0 & 0 & \cdot & \cdot & 0 \\ 0 & 0 & s_{43} & 0 & \cdot & \cdot & 0 \\ \cdot & \cdot & & & & & \cdot \\ \cdot & \cdot & & & & & \cdot \\ 0 & 0 & 0 & 0 & 0 & s_{n,n-1} & 0 \end{bmatrix}$$

The location of the survival rates in the matrix is determined by the need to estimate the number of people who will reach the next age group. Hence the only non-zero terms in the matrix lie on the sub-diagonal. If an estimate is required of the number of survivors reaching the next but one age group it would be necessary to locate the only non-zero terms on the diagonal immediately below that used in the previous calculation.

The birth component of the matrix operator will take the following form:

$$\mathop{\mathbf{F}}_{n \times n} = \begin{bmatrix} 0 & 0 & f_{13} & f_{14} & f_{15} & . & 0 \\ 0 & 0 & & & & & 0 \\ 0 & 0 & & & & & . \\ . & & & & & & \\ . & & & & & & . \\ . & & & & & & \\ 0 & . & . & . & . & . & 0 \end{bmatrix}$$

In this case the only non-zero elements in the matrix will be located in those parts of the first row which correspond to the child-bearing age groups.

The calculation incorporating the matrix operator $\mathbf{G}$ which combines both components of change will be:

$$\underbrace{\begin{bmatrix} 0 & 0 & f_{13} & f_{14} & f_{15} & . & & 0 \\ s_{21} & 0 & 0 & 0 & . & . & & . \\ 0 & s_{32} & 0 & 0 & . & . & & . \\ 0 & 0 & s_{43} & 0 & . & . & & . \\ . & & & & & . & & \\ . & & & & & & & \\ 0 & 0 & . & . & . & s_{n,n-1} & 0 \end{bmatrix}}_{\mathbf{G}} \underbrace{\begin{bmatrix} p_1 \\ p_2 \\ p_3 \\ p_4 \\ . \\ . \\ p_n \end{bmatrix}}_{\mathbf{p}^{(t)}} = \underbrace{\begin{bmatrix} p_1 \\ p_2 \\ p_3 \\ p_4 \\ . \\ . \\ p_n \end{bmatrix}}_{\mathbf{p}^{(t+1)}}$$

These ideas can be illustrated by a simple numerical example for five age groups:

$$\underbrace{\begin{bmatrix} 0 & 0.8 & 0.6 & 0 & 0 \\ 0.8 & 0 & 0 & 0 & 0 \\ 0 & 0.8 & 0 & 0 & 0 \\ 0 & 0 & 0.8 & 0 & 0 \\ 0 & 0 & 0 & 0.7 & 0 \end{bmatrix}}_{\mathbf{G}} \underbrace{\begin{bmatrix} 2000 \\ 1500 \\ 1000 \\ 800 \\ 500 \end{bmatrix}}_{\mathbf{p}^{(t)}} = \underbrace{\begin{bmatrix} 1800\ (1200+600) \\ 1600 \\ 1200 \\ 800 \\ 560 \end{bmatrix}}_{\mathbf{p}^{(t+1)}}$$

The same method can also be used to estimate the population at the next point in time $(t+2)$ from the population at $t+1$, if the matrix operator **G** can be defined in terms of the probabilities of giving birth and surviving during this time period. If it is assumed that these probabilities remain the same as those in the first time period, the population at time $t+2$ will be:

$$
\begin{bmatrix}
0 & 0\cdot8 & 0\cdot6 & 0 & 0 \\
0\cdot8 & 0 & 0 & 0 & 0 \\
0 & 0\cdot8 & 0 & 0 & 0 \\
0 & 0 & 0\cdot8 & 0 & 0 \\
0 & 0 & 0 & 0\cdot7 & 0
\end{bmatrix}
\begin{bmatrix}
1800 \\
1600 \\
1200 \\
800 \\
560
\end{bmatrix}
=
\begin{bmatrix}
2000 \\
1440 \\
1280 \\
960 \\
560
\end{bmatrix}
$$

$$\mathbf{G} \qquad \mathbf{p}^{(t+1)} \qquad \mathbf{p}^{(t+2)}$$

If the same assumption is made about the matrix operator **G** between time $t+2$ and time $t+3$, the population at time $t+3$ will be:

$$
\begin{bmatrix}
0 & 0\cdot8 & 0\cdot6 & 0 & 0 \\
0\cdot8 & 0 & 0 & 0 & 0 \\
0 & 0\cdot8 & 0 & 0 & 0 \\
0 & 0 & 0\cdot8 & 0 & 0 \\
0 & 0 & 0 & 0\cdot7 & 0
\end{bmatrix}
\begin{bmatrix}
2000 \\
1440 \\
1280 \\
960 \\
560
\end{bmatrix}
=
\begin{bmatrix}
1920 \\
1600 \\
1152 \\
1024 \\
672
\end{bmatrix}
$$

$$\mathbf{G} \qquad \mathbf{p}^{(t+2)} \qquad \mathbf{p}^{(t+3)}$$

By these means, then, a self generating or recursive model can be developed to estimate future populations on the basis of stated assumptions about the probabilities of giving birth and surviving at each period. The results of these models can be used to analyse the consequences of alternative assumptions about births and survival over time. The consequences, for instance, of an increase in the probabilities of giving birth from 0·8 to 0·9 and from 0·6 to 0·7, in terms of the same initial population would be:

c

Age group	$\mathbf{p}^{(t)}$	$\mathbf{p}^{(t+1)}$	$\mathbf{p}^{(t+2)}$	$\mathbf{p}^{(t+3)}$
1	2000	2050	2280	2372
2	1500	1600	1640	1824
3	1000	1200	1280	1312
4	800	800	960	1024
5	500	560	560	672
Total	5800	6210	6720	7204

The cumulative effect of the higher birth rates can be seen when these results are compared with the population estimated in the initial example. At times $t+1$ and $t+2$ the size of the initial age group that is calculated on the basis of the higher rates is 14 per cent higher than that estimated earlier, but at $t+3$, when the babies 'born' in the first stage have aged sufficiently to produce their own children the difference between the two estimates rises to 24 per cent. Between time $t+2$ and time $t+3$ there is also an important difference in direction between the two estimates: whereas the size of the initial age group fell from 2000 at time $t+2$ to 1920 at time $t+3$ in the lower birth estimate, a rise from 2280 to 2372 is predicted for this period in the high birth estimate.

2 Extensions of the Basic Model

The basic cohort survival model can be extended with only minor modifications to provide estimates for several regions simultaneously, as long as they share the same assumptions about the probabilities of giving birth and survival, as might be the case, if it relates to overall regional or national average rates. For a given number of k regions, it is only necessary to replace the $n \times 1$ column vectors $\mathbf{p}^{(t)}$ and $\mathbf{p}^{(t+1)}$ by the $n \times k$ matrices $\mathbf{P}^{(t)}$ and $\mathbf{P}^{(t+1)}$. In these matrices the row elements will indicate age distribution and the column elements will refer to regions. The extended model will be:

$$\mathbf{GP}^{(t)} = \mathbf{P}^{(t+1)} \tag{2.4}$$

For a numerical example consisting of two additional regions to the region considered in the initial description it will be:

$$\begin{bmatrix} 0 & 0\cdot8 & 0\cdot6 & 0 & 0 \\ 0\cdot8 & 0 & 0 & 0 & 0 \\ 0 & 0\cdot8 & 0 & 0 & 0 \\ 0 & 0 & 0\cdot8 & 0 & 0 \\ 0 & 0 & 0 & 0\cdot7 & 0 \end{bmatrix} \begin{bmatrix} 2000 & 400 & 1000 \\ 1500 & 300 & 1000 \\ 1000 & 250 & 900 \\ 800 & 200 & 900 \\ 500 & 150 & 600 \end{bmatrix} = \begin{bmatrix} 1800 & 390 & 1340 \\ 1600 & 320 & 800 \\ 1200 & 240 & 800 \\ 800 & 200 & 720 \\ 560 & 140 & 630 \end{bmatrix}$$

$$\mathbf{G} \qquad\qquad \mathbf{P}^{(t)} \qquad\qquad \mathbf{P}^{(t+1)}$$

Only a minor modification is required to incorporate the effects of net migration in this model. In matrix notation the net movement of population in each of the n age groups during the time period under consideration can be expressed as an $n \times 1$ column vector $\mathbf{m}$, and the initial model can be extended so that

$$\mathbf{G}\mathbf{p}^{(t)} + \mathbf{m} = \mathbf{p}^{(t+1)} \tag{2.5}$$

where $\mathbf{G}$ is the $n \times n$ matrix operator expressing the probabilities of giving birth and survival for each of the n age groups between time t and time $t+1$

      $\mathbf{p}^{(t)}$ is an $n \times 1$ column vector of the population in each age group at time t

      $\mathbf{p}^{(t+1)}$ is an $n \times 1$ column vector of the population in each age group at time $t+1$

      $\mathbf{m}$ is an $n \times 1$ column vector expressing, in absolute terms the net migration of population for each age group between time t and time $t+1$

Given net migration estimates of -150, $+200$, $+50$, -50, and -20 for each age group in the initial example, the extended model would be:

$$\begin{bmatrix} 0 & 0\cdot8 & 0\cdot6 & 0 & 0 \\ 0\cdot8 & 0 & 0 & 0 & 0 \\ 0 & 0\cdot8 & 0 & 0 & 0 \\ 0 & 0 & 0\cdot8 & 0 & 0 \\ 0 & 0 & 0 & 0\cdot7 & 0 \end{bmatrix} \begin{bmatrix} 2000 \\ 1500 \\ 1000 \\ 800 \\ 500 \end{bmatrix} + \begin{bmatrix} -150 \\ +200 \\ +50 \\ -50 \\ -20 \end{bmatrix} = \begin{bmatrix} 1650 \\ 1800 \\ 1250 \\ 750 \\ 540 \end{bmatrix}$$

$$\qquad\mathbf{G}\qquad\qquad \mathbf{p}^{(t)}\qquad \mathbf{m}\qquad \mathbf{p}^{(t+1)}$$

For three regions the column vector **m** is replaced by the net migration matrix **M**:

$$\mathbf{G}\mathbf{P}^{(t)} + \mathbf{M} = \mathbf{P}^{(t+1)} \tag{2.6}$$

For a numerical example with three regions and five age groups it will be:

$$\begin{bmatrix} 0 & 0\cdot8 & 0\cdot6 & 0 & 0 \\ 0\cdot8 & 0 & 0 & 0 & 0 \\ 0 & 0\cdot8 & 0 & 0 & 0 \\ 0 & 0 & 0\cdot8 & 0 & 0 \\ 0 & 0 & 0 & 0\cdot7 & 0 \end{bmatrix} \begin{bmatrix} 2000 & 400 & 1000 \\ 1500 & 300 & 1000 \\ 1000 & 250 & 900 \\ 800 & 200 & 900 \\ 500 & 150 & 600 \end{bmatrix} + \begin{bmatrix} -150 & +50 & +100 \\ +200 & -50 & -150 \\ +50 & +50 & -100 \\ -50 & +10 & +40 \\ -20 & +20 & 0 \end{bmatrix}$$

$$= \begin{bmatrix} 1650 & 440 & 1440 \\ 1800 & 270 & 650 \\ 1250 & 290 & 700 \\ 750 & 210 & 760 \\ 540 & 160 & 630 \end{bmatrix}$$

3 The Inter-regional Cohort Survival Model

For a more detailed analysis of migration between regions transition matrices must be constructed for each age group which take account of migration as well as mortality. These express the probability that a person in the nth age group in region i at time t will be in the nth$+1$ age group in region j at time $t+1$, ie:

$$_{n,i}^{(t)}r_{n+1,j}^{(t+1)} = \frac{_{n,i}^{(t)}p_{n+1,j}^{(t+1)}}{p_{n,i}^{(t)}} \tag{2.7}$$

where $_{n,i}^{(t)}r_{n+1,j}^{(t+1)}$ is the probability of a person in the nth age group in region i at time t migrating and surviving into the nth $+1$ age group in region j at time $t+1$

$_{n,i}^{(t)}p_{n+1,j}^{(t+1)}$ is the population of the nth $+1$ age group in region j at time $t+1$ who were in the nth age group in region i at time t

$p_{n,i}^{(t)}$ is the population of the nth age group in region i at time t

The estimation of these transition probabilities is best illustrated by reference to the first age group for the three regions used in the example for the previous section. The gross flows which resulted in the net migration estimates used in that example, can be summarised in a simple table:

		Migration from Region			Total population aged $n+1$ at time $t+1=$ in movement
		1	2	3	
Migration	1	1400	120	280	1800
to	2	100	160	10	270
Region:	3	100	40	510	650
Total out movement		1600	320	800	2720
Deaths		400	80	200	
Total population aged n at time t		2000	400	1000	

This table shows what happened to the initial population between time t and time $t+1$. In the case of the first region, 400 out of the initial total of 2000 died during the period, and, of the survivors 1400 stayed in region 1 while 100 moved to region 2, and 100 moved to region 3. The table also shows the origins of the population in each region at time $t+1$. In the case of the first region, where a total of 1800 people survived to reach the next age group at this date, 1400 were survivors from the initial residents of the region, while 120 were immigrants from region 2 and 280 had moved to region 1 from region 3.

To calculate the matrix of transition probabilities (**R**) each of the population movements in this table must be expressed in terms of the population of each region at time t. Consequently:

$$\mathop{\mathbf{R}}_{k \times k} = \begin{bmatrix} 0.70 & 0.30 & 0.28 \\ 0.05 & 0.40 & 0.01 \\ 0.05 & 0.10 & 0.51 \end{bmatrix}$$

As these probabilities also take mortality into account the sums of the columns must be less than one.

Once the transition probabilities have been estimated for each age group and similar calculations have been made for fertility, matrix operators similar to those used in the basic model can be constructed for each set of inter-regional relationships. These can be handled simultaneously for k regions by a super matrix operator **G** which will consist of $k \times k$ matrices each of which contains $n \times n$ elements relating to the age distribution of population. The inter-relationships involved in the three region case and the resultant super matrix operator will be as shown on the next page.

For projection purposes, as before, this matrix operator is pre-multiplied by a vector of initial population in order to predict the population at time $t + 1$. In this case, however, both vectors will contain $1 \times (n \times 3)$ elements:

$$\mathbf{G P}^{(t)} = \mathbf{P}^{(t+1)} \tag{2.8}$$

Where

$$\mathbf{P}^{(t+1)} = \begin{bmatrix} \mathbf{p}_1 \\ \mathbf{p}_2 \\ \mathbf{p}_3 \end{bmatrix}$$

$$\mathbf{P}^{(t)} = \begin{bmatrix} \mathbf{p}_1 \\ \mathbf{p}_2 \\ \mathbf{p}_3 \end{bmatrix}$$

$$G = \begin{bmatrix} M_{11} & M_{12} & M_{13} \\ M_{21} & M_{22} & M_{23} \\ M_{31} & M_{32} & M_{33} \end{bmatrix}$$

$$G = 3n \times 3n$$

Stayers in region 1	Movers from region 2 to region 1	Movers from region 3 to region 1
Fertility of stayers in region 1	Fertility of movers from region 2 to region 1	Fertility of movers from region 3 to region 1
Movers from region 1 to region 2	Stayers in region 2	Movers from region 3 to region 2
Fertility of movers from region 1 to region 2	Fertility of stayers in region 2	Fertility of movers from region 3 to region 2
Movers from region 1 to region 3	Movers from region 2 to region 3	Stayers in region 3
Fertility of movers from region 1 to region 3	Fertility of movers from region 2 to region 3	Fertility of stayers in region 3

and M_{ij} is a $n \times n$ matrix operator expressing the probabilities that a person living in region j at time t will be living, or will have given birth to a baby who is living in region i at time $t+1$

$p_i^{(t)}$ is a $1 \times n$ vector of the age distribution of the population of region i at time t

$p_i^{(t+1)}$ is a $1 \times n$ vector of the age distribution of the population of region i at time $t+1$

4 Disaggregation and Household Estimation

The disaggregation of the basic cohort survival model involves problems similar to those already discussed in connection with migration. Disaggregation by sex is a simple exercise which can be done either by enlarging the initial matrix or by the creation of growth operators and population vectors which are specific to each sex. In the latter case, it also introduces a straightforward accounting problem with respect to births as it is necessary to distinguish between baby boys and baby girls and amend the first element in each of the population vectors for time $t+1$. In this way the initial equation must be reformulated as follows:

$$G(m)\mathbf{p}(m)^t = \mathbf{p}(m)^{(t+1)} \qquad (2.9)$$
$$G(f)\mathbf{p}(f)^t = \mathbf{p}(f)^{(t+1)}$$

and

$$p(m)_1^{(t+1)}(1-b(f)) = p(m)_1^{(t+1)}$$
$$p(f)_1^{(t+1)}b(f) = p(f)_1^{(t+1)}$$

where m and f refer to males and females respectively

G	is the growth operator
$\mathbf{p}^{(t)}$	is the population at time t
$\mathbf{p}^{(t+1)}$	is the population at time $t+1$
$b(f)$	is the probability of a female birth.

For a five-age-group example, the calculations involved will be:

$$\text{Males} \quad \begin{bmatrix} 0 & 0 & 0 & 0 & 0 \\ 0{\cdot}8 & 0 & 0 & 0 & 0 \\ 0 & 0{\cdot}8 & 0 & 0 & 0 \\ 0 & 0 & 0{\cdot}8 & 0 & 0 \\ 0 & 0 & 0 & 0{\cdot}7 & 0 \end{bmatrix} \begin{bmatrix} 1100 \\ 1000 \\ 900 \\ 800 \\ 600 \end{bmatrix} = \begin{bmatrix} 0 \\ 880 \\ 800 \\ 720 \\ 560 \end{bmatrix}$$

$$\text{Females} \quad \begin{bmatrix} 0 & 0{\cdot}9 & 0{\cdot}8 & 0 & 0 \\ 0{\cdot}9 & 0 & 0 & 0 & 0 \\ 0 & 0{\cdot}9 & 0 & 0 & 0 \\ 0 & 0 & 0{\cdot}9 & 0 & 0 \\ 0 & 0 & 0 & 0{\cdot}8 & 0 \end{bmatrix} \begin{bmatrix} 1000 \\ 1000 \\ 900 \\ 900 \\ 700 \end{bmatrix} = \begin{bmatrix} 1620 \\ 900 \\ 900 \\ 810 \\ 810 \end{bmatrix}$$

If the probability of a female birth is $0{\cdot}5$, the first element in the male vector $\mathbf{p}^{(t+1)}$ will be 810 (ie, $1620 \times (1-0{\cdot}5)$) and the first element in the female vector $\mathbf{p}^{(t+1)}$ will be 810 (in this case $1620 \times 0{\cdot}5$). Consequently, the final estimates for the vector $\mathbf{p}^{(t+1)}$ will be respectively:

$$
\text{Males} = \begin{bmatrix} 810 \\ 880 \\ 800 \\ 720 \\ 560 \end{bmatrix} \qquad \text{Females} = \begin{bmatrix} 810 \\ 900 \\ 900 \\ 810 \\ 810 \end{bmatrix}
$$

Having separated the sexes and introduced a system for differentiating between births, the process of disaggregation by marital status can be expressed in the same way as the process of interaction in the extended migration model. In this case the change of state involved is not the change of address resulting from a move from region i to region j, but it is instead the change in marital status from i to status j. By these means changes in status can be handled through the estimation of transition matrices which express the combined probability of survival and change in state. For each sex, these transition probabilities can then be combined to make up a super matrix operator $\mathbf{G}$ which is premultiplied by the super vector $\mathbf{P}^{(t)}$ to calculate $\mathbf{P}^{(t+1)}$. The elements of the matrix operator in this case will be for single, married, widowed, and divorced status respectively:

$\mathbf{G} =$
$4n \times 4n$

Survive and remain single	Not likely	Not likely	Not likely
Survive and move from single to married	Survive and remain married	Survive and move from widowed to married	Survive and move from divorced to married
Not likely	Survive and move from married to widowed	Survive and remain widowed	Not likely
Not likely	Survive and move from married to divorced	Not likely	Survive and remain divorced

The column elements of this super matrix will refer to the marital status at time t whereas the row elements will refer to the marital status at time $t+1$. The probabilities of births relative to each marital status will now be expressed in the first element of each sub-matrix of the super matrix for females.

Although they can be treated in a similar way to the movement of population between regions, these changes in state introduce a new kind of problem concerning the internal consistency of the model. Logically, the total number of married men that is predicted by the model should be equal to the total number of married women. This condition imposes a constraint on the predicted estimates which must be satisfied in addition to the conditions that are implicit in the initial calculation of the probabilities. To meet this condition a scaling device will be required to adjust the initial estimates for time $t+1$. If this kind of device is used it should be borne in mind that there will be some difference between the probabilities used in the growth operator and the probabilities that are implicit in the results of the model.

Population estimates by age, sex, and marital status can be converted into estimates of potential households by the use of the concept of the headship rate. This expresses the probability that an individual whose age, sex, and marital status can be defined will be a head of household at time $t+1$, ie:

$$r_{nk} = \frac{h_{nk}}{p_{nk}} \tag{2.10}$$

where r_{nk} is the probability that a person in the nth age group of marital status k at time $t+1$ will be a head of household

     h_{nk} is the number of heads of households in the nth age group of marital status k at time $t+1$

     p_{nk} is the total population in the nth age group of marital status k at time $t+1$

These probabilities can be expressed in a row vector $\mathbf{h}^{(t+1)}$ which will estimate the total number of households $(\mathbf{x})$ in the population when multiplied by the age distribution column vector $\mathbf{p}^{(t+1)}$:

$$\mathbf{h}^{(t+1)}\mathbf{p}^{(t+1)} = \mathbf{x} \tag{2.11}$$

In numerical terms for four age/sex/marital status groups the number of households will be:

$$[0\cdot5 \quad 0\cdot1 \quad 0\cdot2 \quad 0\cdot3] \begin{bmatrix} 1000 \\ 900 \\ 800 \\ 600 \end{bmatrix} = [930]$$

$$\mathbf{h}^{(t+1)} \qquad\qquad \mathbf{p}^{(t+1)} \qquad \mathbf{x}$$

5 General Principles Governing the use of Population Models in Planning Studies

The models illustrate the techniques used to analyse and to project the age distribution of a population on the basis of stated assumptions about the probabilities of birth, survival, migration, and/or change in marital status during the projection period. As these probabilities are not fixed in any way, the accuracy of the projections will be largely dependent on the extent to which they can be predicted successfully. For this reason it is important to understand the assumptions and limitations that are implicit in the predicted rates which are used in the projection process.

In most cases the process of population projection involves little more than analysing the nature of past trends for each component of change in the model and extrapolating them. Generally predictions are made on the assumption that population growth is a self-contained process, and that no significant changes will occur in social, environmental or economic factors during the period that is under consideration. In this way the possibility of a dramatic event such as war or an earthquake, and also the effects of gradual changes in attitudes, environment or economic circumstances are largely excluded from these models.

The limitations of these assumptions are most marked in relation to the estimation of migration probabilities and headship rates, both of which are strongly influenced by economic and environmental factors as well as by demographic processes. In these cases it will often be necessary to develop ancillary models within the population analysis to explore the relationships between these factors and population growth.

Further Reading

Apart from internal migration, the basic elements of population change are dealt with at length in the wide range of textbooks that is available on the subject of demography. Good examples of these are to be found in Peterson (1969) and Spiegelman (1969) while Benjamin (1968) deals largely with British sources. Spiegelman's book, (pp 393–422), in particular, includes a useful review of projection methods and an extensive bibliography. On the whole these textbooks are largely descriptive and readers looking for a more mathematical treatment of population processes are advised to consult Keyfitz (1968) or Beshers (1967). The latter is an interesting example of the use of mathematical methods to explore some of the broader aspects of population processes in terms of social systems. Its appendix on quantitative methods (pp 183–202) should be of general interest to most readers.

None of the standard works on demography deal adequately with internal migration. Several studies are available which discuss the models that can be used for analytical purposes as well as the basic elements involved. Useful general reviews with special reference to model building can be found in Olsson (1965) and Willis (1968), while Welch (1971) discusses data sources and estimation techniques with particular reference to British experience.

The analytical methods that are described above are based largely on the work of Keyfitz (1964) and Rogers (1966 and 1968). These contain a more extended discussion of the problems involved in these models and the ways in which they can be extended to serve other purposes. Rogers (1968) is particularly interesting in this respect as it also illustrates some of the estimation problems involved in this kind of study by reference to worked examples for California. Some of the practical problems involved in this work are also discussed in Thompson (1968).

Further study in this general field should also take account of the methods that are used by the government agencies responsible for making population projections for national and local areas. A useful starting point for American literature on this topic is the description of the assumptions underlying the projections made by the Bureau of the Census (1966), while the procedures used for projecting growth patterns within British regions are described in a Ministry of Housing and Local Government publication (1970). This document also contains a detailed explanation of the headship rate methods used by this agency (pp 33–41). A more general review of the population projection methods that are used by a variety of agencies can be found in the relevant United Nations manual on estimating population (United Nations, 1956).

Further studies should also take account of alternative approaches to the cohort survival model that have been developed by researchers in the population field. The most interesting of these from the planning point of view involves the simulation of the behaviour of individual and household units within the population as a whole. By these means internal inconsistencies of the kind described above in relation to disaggregation can be avoided and it is possible to explore the ways in which individuals and households respond to particular sets of economic and social circumstance. The most comprehensive model of this kind is the simulation model developed by Orcutt, Greenberger, Korbel and Rivlin (1961) for their micro analysis of socio-economic systems in the United States between 1950 and 1960. A similar approach has been used by Sheps and her colleagues (Ridley and Sheps, 1966) in their analysis of the demographic and biological aspects of human reproduction.

3. Economic Activity

Some basic techniques for analysing economic activity in relation to urban and regional planning are discussed in this section. The results of this kind of analysis are of basic importance in the formulation of all kinds of planning policies as they indicate the structure and vitality of the local economy, and give insight into the ways in which regions and urban areas developed to their present state and the extent to which these factors are likely to influence their future development.

Analyses of this kind will give an indication of the factors that are responsible for the total wealth of the region or urban area and the distribution of incomes between different sections of the community. They will show the ways in which scarce resources of land, labour, and capital are disposed by market forces and public policies in a mixed economy, and define the limits that are imposed on direct action by planning agencies at each point in time. In this way they establish a framework for a wide range of decisions that must be taken at all levels of planning. The vitality of the economy will be reflected in plans for industrial expansion and for commercial developments such as offices and shopping facilities. These in turn affect the range of employment opportunities that is available to the local population, and the earnings of the workers will be a major factor governing the level of demand for the goods and services that are produced by local industrialists and entrepreneurs.

Urban and regional planners are mainly interested in three distinct aspects of economic activity. Firstly, they are vitally interested in the prospects for a local economy and the ways in which these will be reflected in the scale and character of future development. Secondly, they are concerned with assessing the implications of changes in personal incomes on planning policies. They may extend from an examination of the effect that a rise in personal incomes will have on the demands for local services or transportation facilities to an investigation of their consequences on local housing markets and welfare services. Thirdly, planners are also interested in the implications of changes in economic activity in terms of land, buildings, and channels of communication including basic utility systems such as water supply and sewage facilities. In the formulation of policies for the physical development of land or utility systems they must take account of the new demands that are likely to occur as a result of economic growth.

The models that are developed for, or by, urban and regional planners to analyse economic activity should reflect these requirements. They should be constructed in such a way that changes in economic structure can be explored over time and forecasts of future prospects can be made at the urban or regional level. They should also be conceived in terms of each of the main sectors of the economy and special attention should be given to employment opportunities in relation to the prospects for each industrial sector. Finally, as local economic activity must compete with other regions for limited supplies of capital and mobile population, any analytical model should also be capable of development in such a way that the prospects for the area under consideration can be examined in relation to the prospects for other areas and for the country as a whole.

The analytical models that are developed for these purposes will be used largely to provide information which is required for a wide range of physical planning decisions. Consequently the general emphasis of these models will be different from similar models which are used by economic planners in the formulation of macro economic policies. Like the previous one, the remainder of this chapter is divided into two parts dealing respectively with the basic elements needing consideration, and the two main analytical models that have been used in empirical work.

Basic Elements

Three main elements of economic activity need to be considered in the models that are developed by urban and regional planners for economic analysis and projection. These are the factors governing income, the inter-relationships between industries, and the factors governing employment. In the case of income it is necessary to consider the ways in which the interactions between production, consumption, and investment are expressed in a system of regional accounts. Then the interactions between industries are examined in the context of the input-output table. Finally, employment will be considered in relation to population as well as to output.

1 *Regional Accounts*

The analysis of income at national or regional level presents some fundamental problems of both definition and measurement. Most of the problems of definition can be related to the accounting procedure that must be set up to record the transactions which contribute to the total income. Each of these transactions involves an exchange between a buyer and a seller. For instance, producers exchange their goods in return for the consumer's money, and consumers obtain money to purchase goods by providing their labour in exchange for wages from producers. However, not every transaction contributes to the total income, for goods are often purchased by other producers to use in the manufacture of other goods. Consequently it is necessary to distinguish between intermediate demands of this kind and final demands in the rest of an economy. The value of the national or regional income that is recorded in these accounts, then, represents the total sum of money derived by producers from transactions with the final demand sectors of an economy. Similarly, it can be viewed as the total costs of producing these goods. In the first instance, it takes the form of an expenditure account, and in the second, an income account.

Table 3.1 illustrates the main elements of the national income and expenditure accounts for the United Kingdom in respect of three selected years. The expenditure account records the amount of money

TABLE 3.1

Gross National Product of the United Kingdom 1958–1968

	(£ *million*)		
EXPENDITURE	1958	1963	1968
Consumers' expenditure	15 386	20 141	27 065
Public authority expenditure	3673	5083	7702
Savings: increases in fixed capital and stocks	3603	5131	8002
Domestic Expenditure	22 662	30 355	42 769
Exports and property income from abroad	5837	7249	10 670
Imports and property income paid abroad	− 5420	− 6987	− 10 679
Taxes on expenditure	− 3040	− 4048	− 6960
Subsidies	385	560	886
Gross National Product at Factor Cost	20 424	27 129	36 686
FACTOR INCOMES			
Income from employment	15 250	20 348	28 107
Gross profits of companies	3505	5067	6580
Rent	1061	1526	2359
Total Domestic Income	19 816	26 941	37 046
Stock appreciation	5	− 212	− 650
Residual error	309	− 2	− 129
Gross Domestic Product at Factor Cost	20 130	26 727	36 267
Net property income from abroad	294	402	419
Gross National Product	20 424	27 129	36 686
Capital consumption	1791	2318	3375
National Income	18 633	24 811	33 311

Source: Central Statistical Office: *Annual Abstract of Statistics* No. 104, 1967 table 296, no. 106, 1969 table 296.

Note: Incomes from profits and rent exclude provision for depreciation and stock appreciation.

D

spent by public and private consumers on goods and services together with the increases in stocks that are held by the manufacturers and the formation of fixed capital assets. These items constitute domestic expenditure. Together with the net gain after imports have been considered in relation to exports, and taxes on expenditure offset against subsidies, they make up the Gross National Product, which in 1963 amounted to £27 129 million.

The factor incomes account which provides the basis for the estimation of Gross Domestic Product consists of three items: income from employment, the profits of public and private enterprise, and rent. In this account provision must also be made for stock appreciation or depreciation. The Gross Domestic Product differs from the Gross National Product in that the latter also contains an allowance for the net income derived from property abroad. In either the income or the expenditure accounts the total value of the National Income can be calculated by subtracting the amount that is required to keep real capital intact from the Gross National Product. In 1963 the National Income was estimated at £24 811 million.

As each transaction involves at least two individuals and must be recorded in both the income account and the expenditure account it is convenient to summarise the main elements of regional as well as national accounts by means of a matrix whose row elements refer to income and whose column elements refer to expenditure (see facing page). This matrix shows the transactions that take place between four main kinds of activity, production, consumption, investment, and transactions between the region under consideration and the rest of the country as well as other areas which can be termed generally, the rest of the world. Separate sets of accounts can be prepared for each activity which express its relationships with the other activities. The income elements of the production account consist of consumers' expenditure, capital formation in terms of stocks, new buildings, and equipment, and the revenue from exports while the expenditure elements consist of payments in the form of wages, profits, and rent, provision for the depreciation of existing capital in terms of stocks, buildings, and equipment, and payments for imports. The consumption income account is derived from wages, profits, and rent from the rest of the world as well as from the region, while consumers' expenditure takes the form of payments for goods and services, savings, and expenditure outside the region. Similarly the investment account

Expenditure by:

		Producers	Consumers	Investors	Rest of the world
Income to:	Producers	0	Payments for goods and services	Investment in capital assets (capital formation)	Payments for exports
	Consumers	Wages and profits of factors of production	0	0	Wages and profits earned outside the region
	Investors	Provision for depreciation	Saving	0	Imports of capital from outside the region
	Rest of the world	Payments for imports	Consumers expenditure outside the region	Investment outside the region	0

regards savings, provision for depreciation, and transfers of outside capital to the region as income and capital formation and investment outside the region as expenditure.

Most of the entries for this matrix can be found for the United Kingdom as a whole in table 3.1. In this table a distinction is made between consumers in terms of private expenditure and public authority expenditure, and savings are combined with increases in fixed capital and stocks. Both exports and imports are treated, together with property income in the expenditure accounts, and special sets of accounts are listed in connection with taxes on expenditure and subsidies, while incomes, profits, and rents are recorded in the income accounts, as is stock appreciation.

The dangers of naïve extrapolations of economic activity can also be seen from this table. Between 1963 and 1968, for instance, the Gross Domestic Product increased by more than 35 per cent at current prices. After allowance is made for changes in prices during the five-year period there is still an increase in output of over 15 per cent (table 3.2). At this rate, then, the volume of output could be expected to increase

TABLE 3.2

United Kingdom Gross Domestic Product at factor cost

	Change in G.D.P. at base year factor cost:					
	1958	1959	1960	1961	1962	1963
1958 base	100·0	103·5	108·7	112·7	113·8	118·5
	1963	1964	1965	1966	1967	1968
1963 base	100·0	105·2	107·9	110·0	111·8	115·0

Source: Annual Abstract of Statistics, 1968, 1969.

by 75 per cent over a twenty-year period (ie, $1·15^4$) if allowance is made for the compound nature of growth. Under these circumstances even small changes in the rate of growth in output would give rise to considerable differences over periods of the order of twenty years. Between 1958 and 1963 the Gross Domestic Product rose by 18·5 per cent as against 15·0 per cent between 1963 and 1968. This would lead to an increase of nearly 100 per cent (ie, $1·185^4$) over a twenty-year period as against an increase of only 75 per cent for the slower rate.

The extrapolation problem is further complicated by periodic fluctuations in the rate of growth. The annual changes in Gross Domestic Product at factor cost for the two five-year periods discussed

above are summarised in table 3.2. This shows that the annual increments in terms of a base year index, for the earlier period are 3·5, 5·2,
4·0, 1·1, and 4·7 respectively, as against 5·2, 2·7, 2·1, 1·8, and 3·2 in the
later period. With a range extending from 1·1 to 5·2 in the first period
and from 1·8 to 5·2 in the second, it will be evident that considerable
variations can occur in these extrapolations solely as a result of the
choice of the base year or time period. In cases such as consumer
demand where these fluctuations are further complicated by seasonal
variations considerable ingenuity may be required to determine any
trend from these figures.

2   Inter-Industry Relationships

The structure of intermediate demands in terms of the relationships
between industrial sectors needs to be considered as well as those
between production, consumption, and investment. These inter-
industry relationships can be expressed in a matrix which shows the
transactions between industries as well as between production and
consumption and investment. The resulting matrix is an elaboration of
the accounting matrix that was described above, and for three industries
takes the form shown on the next page.

The entry a_{12} in this matrix indicates the purchases made by industry Y
of the products of industry X, while a_{21} shows the purchases that are
made by industry X of products from industry Y. These transactions
can be expressed not only in terms of income and expenditure but also
as inputs and outputs. In this way a_{12} will express the output of industry
X that is used as an input to industry Y and a_{21} shows the input to
industry X from industry Y. Consequently the column elements of the
table will express inputs while the row elements indicate outputs. In
this way the purchases that are made by each industry from labour,
capital, and the rest of the world can be seen as primary inputs whereas
the sales of the products of each industry to consumption, investment,
and the rest of the world become final outputs or final demand.

Because of the number of inter-relationships involved the input–
output table is best illustrated by reference to national rather than

inter-regional tables. The input–output table that was constructed for the United Kingdom in 1963 illustrates the principles underlying the system described above (table 3.3). It summarises the relationships between 15 industrial sectors in rows 1 to 15 and columns 1 to 15, the interactions between each industry and the main components of final demand in columns 17 to 21 and the relationships between each industry and primary inputs in rows 17 to 21.

Sales by	Purchases by	Industry			Final demand			Gross output
		X	Y	Z	Consumption	Investment	Export	
Industry	X	0	a_{12}	a_{13}	a_{14}	a_{15}	a_{16}	$\Sigma_j a_{1j}$
	Y	a_{21}	0	a_{23}	a_{24}	a_{25}	a_{26}	$\Sigma_j a_{2j}$
	Z	a_{31}	a_{32}	0	a_{34}	a_{35}	a_{36}	$\Sigma_j a_{3j}$
Primary inputs	Consumption	a_{41}	a_{42}	a_{43}	0	0	a_{46}	$\Sigma_j a_{4j}$
	Investment	a_{51}	a_{52}	a_{53}	a_{54}	0	a_{56}	$\Sigma_j a_{5j}$
	Imports	a_{61}	a_{62}	a_{63}	a_{64}	a_{65}	0	$\Sigma_j a_{6j}$
Gross input		$\Sigma_i a_{i1}$	$\Sigma_i a_{i2}$	$\Sigma_i a_{i3}$	$\Sigma_i a_{i4}$	$\Sigma_i a_{i5}$	$\Sigma_i a_{i6}$	$\Sigma_i \Sigma_j a_{ij}$

The descriptive properties of table 3.3 can be seen by reference to a single industry. In 1963 agricultural industries purchased £1694 million worth of inputs. About half these inputs consisted of purchases from other industries (£841 million) and the remainder purchases of primary inputs such as labour. The main inputs from other industries were from food, drink, and tobacco which also includes animal food production, and services where agricultural producers bought £315 million and £281 million worth of products respectively. In contrast to the inputs most of the output of this sector went to final demand, mainly in the form of purchases by private consumers of agricultural products and only £617 million worth of goods was sold to other industries. Most of these goods were sold to the food, drink, and tobacco industry for further processing.

Tables of this kind reveal differences in the structure of industries which are of considerable importance in regional economic analysis. They show those industries that function largely as suppliers to other industries and those industries that exist to supply final demand. For instance, more than three-quarters of the output of the metal manufacturing industry was consumed by other industries whereas less than a tenth of the output of the construction industry was consumed in this way, mainly because construction is regarded as a capital investment. Conversely these tables indicate basic differences in primary inputs to the production process and provide a means of comparing industries in terms of labour costs and profitability.

There should be little difficulty in distinguishing the elements of the Gross Domestic Product in 1963 that were described earlier in table 3.1. In terms of income it will consist of the total income from employment (the sum of row 18) plus the gross profits of companies before depreciation has been taken into account (the sum of row 19). This produces £26 727 million (ie, 18 145 + 8582). In terms of expenditure the Gross Domestic Product will consist of current expenditure (the sum of columns 17 and 18), capital formation (the sum of columns 19 and 20), less the net balance of imports and exports (the sum of column 21 minus the sum of row 20) and taxes (the sum of row 17). As before the total will be £26 727 million (ie, (20 141 + 5083) + (4903 + 228) − (5824 − 5964) − 3488).

The dangers of naïve extrapolations on the basis of data of this kind are considerably increased when separate estimates are required for individual industries. These are illustrated in table 3.4 which shows the changes in output of selected industries for the two periods discussed in the preceding section. The rate of change in these industries varies from up to twice the average rate of growth in manufacturing for chemicals and electrical engineering to an absolute decline in the

TABLE 3.3   United Kingdom: provisional Input-output Transactions Matrix, 1963

Sales by \ Purchases by		Agriculture, forestry, and fishing	Coal mining	Other mining and quarrying	Food, drink, and tobacco	Mineral oil refining	Other chemicals and allied industries	Metal manufacture	Vehicles (including aircraft) and shipbuilding	Other engineering	Textiles, leather, and clothing
		1	2	3	4	5	6	7	8	9	10
Agriculture, forestry, and fishing	1	—	5	—	571	—	—	—	—	—	28
Coal mining	2	1	—	1	14	—	156	12	5	9	16
Other mining and quarrying	3	—	—	—	3	2	9	19	—	19	—
Food, drink, and tobacco	4	315	—	—	—	—	35	—	—	—	2
Mineral oil refining	5	19	1	1	9	—	78	20	6	14	7
Other chemicals and allied industries	6	91	9	12	156	48	—	95	69	140	34
Metal manufacture	7	—	48	—	8	—	23	—	374	781	2
Vehicles (including aircraft) and shipbuilding	8	10	1	1	4	—	3	8	—	41	2
Other engineering	9	26	42	14	100	2	83	98	545	—	40
Textiles, leather, and clothing	10	10	8	—	10	—	8	1	21	27	—
Other manufacturing	11	42	49	7	143	12	83	21	198	289	28
Construction	12	30	18	—	12	—	11	8	11	22	7
Gas, electricity, and water	13	16	25	3	42	5	60	60	40	93	35
Services	14	281	40	51	404	84	232	212	247	510	148
Public administration etc (1)	15	—	—	—	—	—	—	—	—	—	—
Intermediate input (1 to 15)	16	841	246	90	1476	153	781	554	1516	1945	349
Taxes on expenditure *less* subsidies	17	−252	9	10	59	7	32	37	28	73	28
Income from employment	18	353	535	47	546	25	388	502	890	1877	771
Gross profits and other trading income (2)	19	601	117	34	473	29	312	249	244	714	286
Imports of goods and services	20	151	5	1	507	284	284	315	107	221	436
Sales by final buyers to one another	21	—	—	1	8	—	5	66	22	22	8
Total input (17 to 21)	22	1694	912	183	3069	498	1802	1723	2807	4852	1878

(1) **Public** administration and defence, public health and educational services, ownership of dwellings, domestic households, and services to private non-profit-making bodies serving persons.
(2) Before providing for depreciation but after providing for stock appreciation.
(3) Including Residual error.
Source: Central Statistical Office—*National Income and Expenditure 1967*, table 19, pp 24–25.

£million

Gas, electricity, and water	Services	Public administration etc. (1)	Total intermediate output (1 to 15)	Final buyers					Total final output (17 to 21)	Total output (16 plus 22)	
				Current expenditure		Gross domestic capital formation		Exports			
				Personal sector	Public authorities	Fixed	Stocks				
13	14	15	16	17	18	19	20	21	22	23	
— 345	4 37	— —	617 647	987 208	14 26	9 21	24 −23	43 33	1077 265	1694 912	1 2
—	2	—	166	—	—	—	—	17	17	183	3
—	76	—	431	2290	49	—	56	243	2638	3069	4
30	64	—	287	61	15	8	2	125	211	498	5
22	124	—	1052	244	135	—	−19	390	750	1802	6
29	14	—	1424	—	5	40	−27	281	299	1723	7
2 68	313 217	— —	401 1555	484 353	598 284	437 1322	67 81	820 1257	2406 3297	2807 4852	8 9
—	42	—	208	1145	37	—	15	473	1670	1878	10
25 8	647 118	— —	2009 259	631 387	151 303	42 2170	13 21	318 10	1155 2891	3164 3150	11 12
— 160	236 —	— —	707 2981	653 6787	81 742	158 437	— 2	4 1473	896 9441	1603 12 422	13 14
—	—	—	—	1440	2732	—	—	—	4172	4172	15
689	1894	—	12 744	15 670	5172	4644	212	5487	31 185	43 929	16
69	412	—	637	2648	91	112	—	—	2851	3488	17
373	6242	3063	18 145	—	—	—	—	—	—	18 145	18
455	3 120(3)	1109	8582	—	—	—	—	—	—	8582	19
17	680	—	3602	1656	186	242	16	262	2362	5964	20
—	74	—	219	167	−366	−95	—	75	−219	—	21
1603	12 422	4172	43 929	20 141	5083	4903	228	5824	36 179	80 108	22

output of shipbuilding and marine engineering industries. If extra-polated for a twenty-year period the extreme values in this table would estimate a growth of nearly 300 per cent in the case of chemicals (ie, $1 \cdot 404^4$) and a decline in ship-building to only one-third of its output level in 1958 ($0 \cdot 774^4$) as against an average increase of about 100 per cent for manufacturing as a whole.

TABLE 3.4

United Kingdom Index of Industrial Production changes in selected industries, 1958–63 and 1963–8

1958 *Factor Cost*	1958	1959	1960	1961	1962	1963
Chemicals and allied industries	100·0	111·3	123·4	124·9	130·4	140·4
Electrical engineering	100·0	110·4	115·9	120·0	125·9	134·1
Shipbuilding and marine engineering	100·0	93·6	84·8	85·7	86·6	77·4
Textiles	100·0	105·6	110·4	106·6	104·6	109·6
Clothing and footwear	100·0	111·5	119·6	121·9	118·1	120·0
All manufacturing	100·0	106·0	114·6	114·8	115·3	120·0
1963 *Factor Cost*	1963	1964	1965	1966	1967	1968
Chemicals and allied industries	100·0	109·8	117·1	123·4	130·4	139·8
Electrical engineering	100·0	110·7	110·3	120·3	127·5	136·9
Shipbuilding and marine engineering	100·0	96·6	95·5	93·2	90·0	86·8
Textiles	100·0	105·7	108·3	107·6	105·0	119·1
Clothing and footwear	100·0	104·3	106·9	105·8	101·5	103·7
All manufacturing	100·0	108·9	112·5	114·2	114·0	121·2

Source: *Annual Abstract of Statistics*, 1965 and 1969.

Apart from this range of variation, the difficulties of extrapolation are increased by fluctuations within industries. The output of clothing and footwear, for instance, increased by only 3·7 per cent between 1963 and 1968 as against 20 per cent between 1958 and 1963. Similarly the rate of growth in the output of textiles in the later period was twice as great as that of the earlier period. However, in the later period itself there were marked fluctuations in this industry from year to year in that the annual increments of change were $+5\cdot7$, $+2\cdot6$, $-0\cdot7$, $-2\cdot6$, and $+14\cdot1$ respectively in terms of the base year index.

3 Employment

Estimates of employment are related to regional accounting systems and inter-industry input output tables by means of the wages and salaries that are recorded in the income accounts or by some measure of productivity. This measure of productivity generally expresses the net output per person employed in relation to a single industry or to the economy as a whole. Given, then, that the value of the net output of the manufacturing industries estimated by the Census of Production in 1963 was £10 848 million, and that it was produced by a labour force consisting of 7·95 million, the average productivity or net output per head would be £1364 (ie, 10 848/7·95) (table 3.5).

Employment estimates must also be considered in terms of a labour force which is drawn from certain sections of the population as a whole. The relationship between the labour force and the population of working age is generally measured by an activity rate. This expresses the proportion of the population under consideration that is in employment. In 1963, for instance, 25·7 million people in the United Kingdom out of an estimated home population of 41·3 million aged 15 or over were included in the working population. In this case then the activity rate would be 0·62 (ie, 25·7/41·3) (table 3.6).

Even in large regions projections of employment in individual industries are liable to fluctuate considerably during the time periods envisaged in most planning studies. These fluctuations will reflect not only changes in the level of output in the industries concerned but also changes in productivity resulting from technological innovation and alterations in the composition of the labour force. The effect of these relationships is illustrated for the United Kingdom as a whole in table 3.5 which shows the changes that took place in output, productivity, and employment for three industries between 1963 and 1968. From this table it can be seen that there is no simple correlation between changes in output and changes in employment particularly when these are viewed in terms of the average rate of change in all manufacturing industries. In the chemical industry, for example, the level of employ-

TABLE 3.5

United Kingdom net output, persons employed and net output per person employed in selected industries 1963 and 1968

	1963	1968	*Change 1963–8 relative to change in all manufacturing*
Chemicals and allied industries			
Net output (£ million)	1094	1571	97·3
Average employment (000)	470	453	94·9
Net output per person employed (£)	2328	3468	102·5
Engineering and allied industries			
Net output (£ million)	4453	6669	101·5
Average employment (000)	3393	3503	101·6
Net output per person employed (£)	1312	1904	99·9
Textiles, leather, and clothing			
Net output (£ million)	1235	1705	93·6
Average employment (000)	1303	1227	92·7
Net output per person employed (£)	948	1390	100·9
All Manufacturing			
Net output (£ million)	10 848	16 012	100·0
Average employment (000)	7952	8077	100·0
Net output per person employed (£)	1364	1982	100·0

Source: *Annual Abstract of Statistics*, 1970, table 155.

ment declined much faster during this period than the relative level of output because levels of productivity were rising faster than levels of output. Conversely, employment in the engineering industries rose considerably during this period relative to the overall average largely because productivity was increasing at a slower rate than output.

Generally, levels of employment change at a slower rate than either output or productivity, even after allowance has been made for changes in prices. As a result the risk of compounding errors when projecting over periods of five years or more is less in respect of employment. However, it should be borne in mind that national figures such as those used above will tend to even out peaks and troughs which are of major importance at the local or regional level. At this level employment figures for individual industries are liable to considerable fluctuations, particularly when estimates refer to a small number of firms. In this case, the prospects of closing down an establishment or opening up a new one may give rise to dramatic changes in employment irrespective of changes in output or productivity.

By comparison with estimates for individual industries estimates of the labour force as a whole show less variation over time, even in small labour market areas, mainly because changes in the size of the population as a whole occur much more slowly than changes in output. This can be seen if table 3.5 is compared to table 3.6 which shows the total working population in relation to the male and female population aged 15 and over in 1965 and 1968. In this period the total number of males and females aged 15 or over rose by 2·1 per cent from 41·3 to 42·1 million while the working population increased by 0·4 per cent from 25·7 to 25·8 million. As the growth in the labour force was less than the growth in population the overall activity rate fell from 0·62 to 0·61 during this period. These overall figures must be considered in relation to the changes for different groups within the population. In this case these show that female employment was rising faster than female population with the result that activity rates were increasing whereas male activity rates were declining as a result of an absolute decline in employment at a time when the population aged 15 and over rose by 2·2 per cent.

Generally local activity rates should reflect regional or national activity rates as long as employment estimates are analysed in relation to the labour market areas involved. However, spatial variations may occur as a result of the employment opportunities that are locally available or the composition of the population of working age. They will tend to be lower in remote areas where opportunities for employ-

TABLE 3.6

United Kingdom: activity rates, 1963 and 1968

	1963	1968	Percentage change 1963–8
Males			
Home population aged 15 and over (000)	19 665	20 098	+2·2
Total working population at mid June (000)	16 942	16 679	−1·6
Activity rate	0·86	0·83	−3·5
Females			
Home population aged 15 and over (000)	21 591	22 011	+1·9
Total working population at mid June (000)	8777	9146	+4·2
Activity rate	0·41	0·42	+2·2
Total			
Home population aged 15 and over (000)	41 256	42 109	+2·1
Total working population at mid June (000)	25 719	25 825	+0·4
Activity rate	0·62	0·61	−1·6

Source: *Annual Abstract of Statistics*, 1964 and 1969.

ment, particularly in respect of female workers, are limited, and they will also tend to be lower in areas with a high proportion of elderly population. Conversely they will be generally higher in areas such as large cities where there are opportunities for subsidiary or part-time employment and in populations containing a relatively large number of unmarried females of working age.

Analytical Models

The main task of the economic models of regions and urban areas that are used for planning purposes is to assess their future prospects in terms of income and employment at certain points in time from basic information in the form of regional accounts, inter-industry input output tables, and employment on the basis of stated assumptions. No standard approach to this task has yet emerged in empirical work, although in his valuable survey of regional economics Meyer found that, it must be recognised that input output and economic base analysis, with all their shortcomings and deficiencies, are the tools almost invariably relied upon at the present time when actual empirical work in regional economics must be performed.' (Meyer, 1963, pp 35–36). These two methods are described in the remainder of this section.

The Export Base Multiplier

The distinction between flows of cash and goods within a region and flows that cross regional boundaries that was made in the regional accounting system is fundamental to the concept of the export base (often called the economic base). This concept assumes that an urban or regional economy can be divided into two sectors: a basic sector (sometimes called an export sector) whose income is derived from transactions which take place across the boundaries of the area under consideration, and a service sector (sometimes called a local or non-basic sector) whose income is derived from transactions within this area. The export base distinguishes between these two sectors by reference to two types of market area: locally produced goods and services which are exported for sale outside the area under consideration would be classified as basic, and locally produced goods and services which are consumed within this area would be considered as belonging to the service sector.

a. *General Methods*   The distinction between basic and service sectors becomes significant as a means of prediction when it is considered within the general context of the multiplier. In economics, the concept of the multiplier refers to the effect that a given increase in expenditure will ultimately have on the increase in national income as a whole. In terms of the export base it generally refers to the ultimate increase in a region's income that results from an increase in the basic sector. In overall terms, the base multiplier would be defined as:

$$K = \frac{Y}{X} \tag{3.1}$$

where K is the multiplier

Y is the regional income

X is the total export income (including net factor payments from abroad and net transfers from abroad)

and $Y = D + X$

where D is the locally derived (service sector) income.

In incremental terms, the multiplier would be

$$K = \frac{\Delta Y}{\Delta X} \tag{3.2}$$

where $\Delta Y = \Delta D + \Delta X$.

The overall concept of the export base multiplier can be illustrated by a simple example for an economy divided into five sectors:

| | £ sales to: | | |
	Local Markets	External Markets	All Markets
Agriculture	8	42	50
Food products	30	30	60
Engineering	15	65	80
Textiles	45	15	60
Services	142	8	150
Total	240	160	400

When the sales in each sector are classified according to their destination it can be seen that the majority of agricultural and engineering sales are to external markets while sales of services and textiles take place largely to local markets and food products are divided equally between markets. In all some £160 out of the total of £400 worth of sales are in external markets. Consequently, the overall multiplier in this case is 2·5 (ie, 400/160).

The export base multiplier implies that basic activities are the essential city building activities in that patterns of growth and decline in towns and regions are determined by patterns of growth and decline in this sector of economy. From this assumption a number of predictive models can be developed, given one of two further assumptions; either that the relationships implicit in the multiplier will remain constant during the time period under consideration; or that changes in the multiplier can be determined by reference to factors outside the model. The common feature of all these models is the assumption that the income of a region as a whole can be predicted solely from a prediction of its basic sector, given some information about the multiplier. In the example above, then, if external sales rose to £200 and the multiplier remained constant at 2·5 the income of the economy as a whole would rise to £500 (ie, 2·5 × 200).

b. *Approaches to Empirical Work* Two distinct approaches have emerged in empirical work on the export base multiplier. It has been the subject of formal economic analysis as a result of the inclusion of income and employment multipliers in aggregate economic theory and

E

it has also been a subject of interest to geographers and planners. Beginning with the pioneer work of Hildrebrand and Mace on Los Angeles County which was published in 1950, the economists have been mainly interested in the refinement and interpretation of the crude export base multiplier in terms of economic theory. This work has been linked to the development of inter-regional trade multipliers which deal with flows between several regions rather than flows between one region and the rest of the world. Until recently the work of geographers and planners in this field had proceeded largely independently of that of the economists. Following the work of Homer Hoyt and his associates in the 1930s, it consists largely of empirical studies which are closely related to local planning problems. These studies have often encountered problems of data collection which have led to a reformulation of the export base in terms of employment rather than income and also encouraged the development of indirect methods of defining the export base.

The employment base used by some geographers and planners is a special version of the export base. It differs from the concept of the export base in that certain implicit assumptions are made about the relationship between employment and income within the local economy, and it introduces a number of problems that were not present in income models as procedures must be devised to classify workers into sectors using field survey material or indirect sources such as the Census. Typical rules used in connection with the latter are the location quotient (basic employment defined as the excess employment in local industries where an industry's share of the total employment is greater than the national average) and the minimum requirements method (basic employment defined as the excess employment in local industries where an industry's share of the total employment is greater than an empirically defined minimum related to areal size). In these cases reservations regarding the definition of basic employment must be taken into account as well as the general objections noted below to the method as a whole.

The rules themselves are best illustrated by simple examples for the five-sector case. The location quotient is derived in the following way:

	Employment in study area		National employment	Basic employment = excess % of local employment over national employment
	No.	%	%	
Agriculture	30	12	5·5	6·5
Food products	35	14	18	—
Engineering	50	20	14	6
Textiles	35	14	18	—
Services	100	40	44·5	—
Total	250	100	100	12·5

In this case only agriculture and engineering had a higher local proportion of employment than the national average. If this excess employment is considered as basic the multiplier for the area would be 8 (ie, 100/12·5). The minimum requirements technique can be illustrated by reference to three additional regions X, Y, and Z:

	Percentage employment in:				Minimum observed requirements	Basic employment = excess % of study area employment over minimum requirements
	Study area	Region X	Region Y	Region Z		
Agriculture	12	2	8	14	2	10
Food products	14	16	21	23	14	—
Engineering	20	10	16	11	10	10
Textiles	14	24	17	6	6	8
Services	40	48	38	46	38	2
Total	100	100	100	100	70	30

In this case the proportion of study area employment in textiles and services as well as in agriculture and engineering exceeded the minimum proportions found in the four regions. If this excess employment is considered as basic the multiplier for the area would be 3·3 (ie, 100/30).

c. *Principles Governing the use of the Export Base Multiplier* As a result of the empirical work described above a substantial body of literature has grown up around the concept of the export base multiplier and a number of objections have been raised which must be borne in mind when contemplating the use of this concept in planning studies. These fall into three broad categories concerned with the weakness of the initial assumption about exports being the prime mover of growth, the limitations of the concept as a forecasting device, and the effect of differences in areal size respectively.

Most critics of the concept of the export base argue that, although there may be a general correlation between growth in the export sector and growth in the local economy as a whole, it is a gross over-simplification of reality to postulate that the export sector, even when defined to include net income payments to residents from abroad, is the sole mover of local growth. In particular this concept ignores the effect that flows of goods within the local economy may have on growth. These objections have been summed up by Pfouts in the following terms,

> The economic (export) base theory emphasises an important determinant of income in the community. But it is not the only determinant of income within the community. The flow of income inside the community also generates income and hence community development. It is true that we cannot live by taking in each other's washing, but if nobody is taking in washing, income opportunities are lost and the community is a less pleasant place than it would otherwise be. (Pfouts, 1960, p. 305)

The critics of the export base then argue that, even if the weaknesses of the initial assumptions are overcome, there are a number of serious limitations involved in the use of this concept as a forecasting device. They point out that the concept of the multiplier is usually used in economics in respect of short-term fluctuations and that there is a fundamental difference between problems of this kind and problems of long-term development. The export base multiplier should in no sense then be considered as a substitute for a theory of economic growth at the regional or local level.

There are also considerable differences between the use of this concept at a small town scale and its use at the regional scale. These affect both the numerical value of the multiplier and its usefulness. The size of the export sector varies inversely according to the size of the area involved. In a large region, then, the size of the export sector in relation to the economy as a whole will be small. Consequently, the numerical value of the export base multiplier will be large and the scale of error involved in using this multiplier will also be large. In this case, where the local market is relatively large, inter-industry linkages between service industries are likely to be an important element in local growth. As a result the export base concept will provide a poor explanation for growth in this kind of area. It is likely to be much more useful in small regions where the size of the export sector is relatively large, the numerical value of the multiplier relatively low, and the possibility of internal linkages restricted.

2 *Input–Output Analysis*

Inter-industry input output tables of the kind illustrated in table 3.3 are of little use in themselves for predictive purposes but a number of methods have been devised to use these tables in this way as a result of certain simplifying assumptions about the nature of economic inter-relationships. These methods are usually referred to as input–output analysis. The main objectives of input–output analysis are to estimate multipliers which are broadly similar to those of the export base multiplier but input–output analysis is concerned with the effect that a change in *final demand* as a whole (that is sales to export, consumption and investment sectors) would have on the other industrial sectors of the economy whereas the export base multiplier was concerned only with the effects that a change in the *export sector* would have on the economy as a whole. Input–output analysis, then, stresses the importance of inter-industry relationships in the economy and seeks to answer the following question: given that the final demand for goods and services in an economy at a given point in time is known, what levels of gross output will be required to meet this demand and also take account of the productive activities that are required to create these goods and services?

a. *Basic Methods* The basic methods used in input–output analysis can be illustrated by reference to a simple numerical example involving three industrial sectors (agriculture, manufacturing, and services), an aggregate final demand sector (representing personal consumption, government consumption, and exports) and an aggregate primary input sector (representing factor payments, provision for depreciation, and imports).

£

Purchases by \ Sales by		Industry			Final demand	Gross output
		Agriculture	Manufacturing	Services		
Industry	Agriculture	0	200	100	200	500
	Manufacturing	300	0	300	400	1000
	Services	0	200	0	300	500
Primary input		200	600	100	0	900
Gross input		500	1000	500	900	2900

In this case, then, the agricultural sector sold £500 worth of output. Of these products £200 worth was consumed by the final demand sector, £200 worth by manufacturing and the remaining £100 worth was consumed by the service industries. To produce this output involved the payment of £200 for primary inputs, and £300 to manufacturing industries. Similarly, the manufacturing sector produced £1000 worth of products of which £400 worth was consumed by the final demand sector, and £300 each by agricultural and service sectors. Goods and services worth £1000 had to be purchased for this purpose, of which £600 was spent on primary inputs, and £200 each on the products of the agricultural and service industries.

The first step in the analysis is to construct a table which indicates the amount of input that is required from each industry to produce one unit of output in a given industry. The coefficients derived in this way are usually termed technical coefficients, and are calculated only for the processing sectors of the table. For the agricultural industry, then, in the table above, where a gross output worth £500 required inputs worth £300 from the manufacturing industry, the respective technical co-efficient would be 0·6 (ie, 300/500). Similarly, the technical coefficients for purchases in connection with the manufacturing industry which are entered in the manufacturing industry column would be 0·2 (200/1000), 0, and 0·2 (200/1000) respectively. The complete technical table derived in this way would be:

Purchases by ⟍ Sales by		Industry		
		Agriculture	Manufacturing	Services
Industry	Agriculture	0	0·2	0·2
	Manufacturing	0·6	0	0·6
	Services	0	0·2	0

Using these coefficients the relationships between industries, final demand, and output can be expressed as a set of three simultaneous linear equations:

$$a_{11}x_1 + a_{12}x_2 + a_{13}x_3 + d_1 = x_1 \qquad (3.3a)$$

$$a_{21}x_1 + a_{22}x_2 + a_{23}x_3 + d_2 = x_2 \qquad (3.3b)$$

$$a_{31}x_1 + a_{32}x_2 + a_{33}x_3 + d_3 = x_3 \qquad (3.3c)$$

where a_{ij} is the technical coefficient expressing the input from industry i required to produce a unit of output in industry j.

d_i is the final demand for industry i.

x_i is the gross output of industry i.

In matrix notation this system is reformulated as follows:

$$\mathbf{Ax} + \mathbf{d} = \mathbf{x} \qquad (3.4)$$

$$\text{where } \mathbf{A} = \begin{bmatrix} a_{11} & a_{12} & a_{13} \\ a_{21} & a_{22} & a_{23} \\ a_{31} & a_{32} & a_{33} \end{bmatrix}$$

$$\mathbf{x} = \begin{bmatrix} x_1 \\ x_2 \\ x_3 \end{bmatrix}$$

$$\mathbf{d} = \begin{bmatrix} d_1 \\ d_2 \\ d_3 \end{bmatrix}$$

By using elementary algebra this equation system can be re-arranged so that:

$$\mathbf{d} = \mathbf{x} - \mathbf{A}\mathbf{x} \qquad (3.5)$$

If an identity matrix $\mathbf{I}$, which is the equivalent of a unit multiplier in ordinary mathematics, is introduced then

$$\mathbf{d} = \mathbf{I}\mathbf{x} - \mathbf{A}\mathbf{x} \qquad (3.6)$$

This can be re-arranged so that:

$$\mathbf{d} = (\mathbf{I} - \mathbf{A})\mathbf{x} \qquad (3.7)$$

The simplest solution to this system is the open solution. This involves multiplying both sides of the equation by the inverse matrix $(\mathbf{I} - \mathbf{A})^{-1}$ so that

$$(\mathbf{I} - \mathbf{A})^{-1} \mathbf{d} = \mathbf{x} \qquad (3.8)$$

By these means, then, the consequences of a given change in the final demand sector in terms of output as a whole can be estimated if it is assumed that the technical coefficients which make up the matrix $\mathbf{A}$ remain constant over time or can be predicted outside the model.

The stages in the solution and some of the uses of the solution can be illustrated by reference to the worked example. In this case:

$$\mathbf{A} = \begin{bmatrix} 0 & 0.2 & 0.2 \\ 0.6 & 0 & 0.6 \\ 0 & 0.2 & 0 \end{bmatrix} \qquad \mathbf{d} = \begin{bmatrix} 200 \\ 400 \\ 300 \end{bmatrix} \qquad \mathbf{x} = \begin{bmatrix} 500 \\ 1000 \\ 500 \end{bmatrix}$$

and

$$I = \begin{bmatrix} 1 & 0 & 0 \\ 0 & 1 & 0 \\ 0 & 0 & 1 \end{bmatrix}$$

The term $(I - A)$ is estimated as follows:

$$\underset{I}{\begin{bmatrix} 1 & 0 & 0 \\ 0 & 1 & 0 \\ 0 & 0 & 1 \end{bmatrix}} - \underset{A}{\begin{bmatrix} 0 & 0.2 & 0.2 \\ 0.6 & 0 & 0.6 \\ 0 & 0.2 & 0 \end{bmatrix}} = \underset{(I-A)}{\begin{bmatrix} 1 & -0.2 & -0.2 \\ -0.6 & 1 & -0.6 \\ 0 & -0.2 & 1 \end{bmatrix}}$$

The inverse of the matrix $(I - A)^{-1}$ is calculated by the method described in appendix A, which gives:

$$(I - A)^{-1} = \begin{bmatrix} 1.196 & 0.326 & 0.435 \\ 0.815 & 1.359 & 0.978 \\ 0.163 & 0.272 & 1.196 \end{bmatrix}$$

The solution can be checked by multiplying out eq (3.8) for the initial values of **d**:

$$\begin{bmatrix} 1.196 & 0.326 & 0.435 \\ 0.815 & 1.359 & 0.978 \\ 0.163 & 0.272 & 1.196 \end{bmatrix} \begin{bmatrix} 200 \\ 400 \\ 300 \end{bmatrix} = \begin{bmatrix} 500 \\ 1000 \\ 500 \end{bmatrix}$$

Given that the values of the technical coefficients are assumed to remain constant it is now possible to use the inverse matrix to estimate the effect of a change in final demand on gross output as a whole. Suppose, then, that the final demand for agricultural goods increases from £200 to £600 (ie, by £400) then the effect on the economy as a whole would be:

$$\begin{bmatrix} 1.196 & 0.326 & 0.435 \\ 0.815 & 1.359 & 0.978 \\ 0.163 & 0.272 & 1.196 \end{bmatrix} \begin{bmatrix} 400 \\ 0 \\ 0 \end{bmatrix} = \begin{bmatrix} 478 \\ 326 \\ 65 \end{bmatrix}$$

In this case an increase in the final demand for agricultural goods of £400 would result in an overall increase in output of £869, of which £478 would be for agricultural goods, (ie, £78 in addition to the initial

£400 in final demand), £326 for manufactured goods, and £65 for services. The crude multiplier for the agricultural sector, then, would be 2·17 (ie, 869/400).

If, on the other hand, there was an increase of £400 in the final demand for manufactured goods then:

$$\begin{bmatrix} 1·196 & 0·326 & 0·435 \\ 0·815 & 1·359 & 0·978 \\ 0·163 & 0·272 & 1·196 \end{bmatrix} \begin{bmatrix} 0 \\ 400 \\ 0 \end{bmatrix} = \begin{bmatrix} 130 \\ 544 \\ 109 \end{bmatrix}$$

In this case there would be an overall increase in output of £783 of which £544 would be for manufactured goods (ie, £144 in addition to the initial £400 in final demand), £130 for agricultural goods, and £109 for services. The crude multiplier for the manufacturing sector, then, would be 1·96 (ie, 783/400). In this example, then, the overall increase in output is greater for a unit increase in the final demand for agricultural products than for manufacturing products, and it might be expected that this would be reflected in policies relating to public authority expenditure.

A more refined version of the multiplier which takes account of the relationships between personal consumption and primary inputs of labour can be estimated by treating these parts of the final demand sector and the primary input sector in the same way as the production sector. In the three industry example described above, the main elements of final demand and primary input must be recorded separately (p. 75). The matrix of technical coefficients (A) for this table will include personal consumption and labour as well as inter-industry relationships:

Purchases by / Sales by	Agriculture	Manufacturing	Services	Personal consumption
Agriculture	0	0·2	0·2	0·2
Manufacturing	0·6	0	0·6	0·2
Services	0	0·2	0	0·6
Labour	0·2	0·3	0·2	0

£

Sales by \ Purchases by		Industry			Final demand		Gross output
		Agriculture	Manufacturing	Services	Personal consumption	Government expenditure and exports	
Industry	Agriculture	0	200	100	100	100	500
	Manufacturing	300	0	300	100	300	1000
	Services	0	200	0	300	0	500
Primary Inputs	Labour	100	300	100	0	0	500
	Imports	100	300	0	0	0	400
Gross input		500	1000	500	500	400	2900

This system can be solved in the same way as before so that the inverse matrix $(\mathbf{I} - \mathbf{A})^{-1}$ is

$$\begin{bmatrix} 1\cdot891 & 1\cdot036 & 1\cdot269 & 1\cdot347 \\ 2\cdot073 & 2\cdot643 & 2\cdot487 & 2\cdot435 \\ 1\cdot153 & 1\cdot282 & 2\cdot383 & 1\cdot917 \\ 1\cdot231 & 1\cdot257 & 1\cdot477 & 2\cdot383 \end{bmatrix}$$

This solution can be checked by multiplying out the initial equation (3.8) where the values of **d** refer in this case only to government expenditures and exports.

$$\begin{bmatrix} 1\cdot891 & 1\cdot036 & 1\cdot269 & 1\cdot347 \\ 2\cdot073 & 2\cdot643 & 2\cdot487 & 2\cdot435 \\ 1\cdot153 & 1\cdot282 & 2\cdot383 & 1\cdot917 \\ 1\cdot231 & 1\cdot257 & 1\cdot477 & 2\cdot383 \end{bmatrix} \begin{bmatrix} 100 \\ 300 \\ 0 \\ 0 \end{bmatrix} = \begin{bmatrix} 500 \\ 1000 \\ 500 \\ 500 \end{bmatrix}$$

Given the values of the technical coefficients the inverse matrix can be used to estimate multipliers for each sector which take account of personal consumption and labour inputs as well as inter-industry relationships. For instance, in agricultural exports or government expenditure of £100 would lead to an overall increase in output of £634, a multiplier of 6·34 (ie, 634/100) as against a crude multiplier of only 2·17 for this sector in the initial model:

$$\begin{bmatrix} 1\cdot891 & 1\cdot036 & 1\cdot269 & 1\cdot347 \\ 2\cdot073 & 2\cdot643 & 2\cdot487 & 2\cdot435 \\ 1\cdot153 & 1\cdot282 & 2\cdot383 & 1\cdot917 \\ 1\cdot231 & 1\cdot257 & 1\cdot477 & 2\cdot383 \end{bmatrix} \begin{bmatrix} 100 \\ 0 \\ 0 \\ 0 \end{bmatrix} = \begin{bmatrix} 189 \\ 207 \\ 115 \\ 123 \end{bmatrix}$$

b. *Regional Input–Output Analysis* Given resources for data collection, inter-industry tables of the type shown in table 3.3 can be prepared for a town or a region as well as for a nation as a whole. In these tables exports and imports will refer to trade between the study area and the rest of the nation as well as to international trade. As exports and imports will account for a much larger proportion of gross inputs and outputs in urban areas or regions than for the nation as a whole, it may be necessary to expand the tables so that external sources and destinations can be specified in greater detail. The simplest method of expansion involves the subdivision of the final demand and primary input columns for this purpose, but this does not affect the relationships which are expressed in the multiplier. A much more elaborate inter-industry table is required for the analysis of the interaction between industries in the area under consideration and industries in the rest of the world. It would take the form of a supermatrix consisting of the following elements:

Inter-industry transactions within the region	Products bought by rest of world industries from regional industries
Products bought by regional industries from rest of world industries	Inter-industry transactions within the rest of world

A table of this kind would increase the number of transactions recorded in the inter-industry table, and the matrix to be inverted, fourfold. Even for the three-sector case described above the number of transactions would be increased from 9 (3 sectors × 3 sectors) to 36 (3 sectors × 2 regions) × (3 sectors × 2 regions).

Where trade between more than two regions is involved serious difficulties will be experienced in the construction of inter-industry tables because of the complexity of the data required. As a result a number of special versions of input–output analysis have been developed for inter-regional studies. These involve either the introduction of further simplifying assumptions to enable inter-regional commodity flows to be predicted by indirect means from aggregate data or the specification of the input–output model in terms of inter-regional trade relationships rather than inter-industry relationships. In this case the technical coefficients of the inter-industry model are replaced by trade coefficients which indicate the amount of input that is required from each region to produce a unit of output in a given region.

c. *Principles Governing the use of Input–Output Analysis* Certain limitations of the basic assumptions underlying input–output analysis must be borne in mind when contemplating the construction of input–output models of regions or urban areas for predictive purposes. Models of this kind can be used for prediction only when externally derived estimates of final demand are available for each industrial sector and the usefulness of the predictions as a whole will depend, to a large extent, on the accuracy of these estimates. The relationship between final demand sectors and the industrial sectors is also more complex in reality than postulated in either of the solutions discussed above. Final demand generally includes expenditure by private consumers, and the main source of income for this purpose is factor payments from industry in the form of wages and profits. Thus the level of private consumption is related to the level of production as a whole which is predicted in the model by estimating final demand, which includes private consumption, independently. This kind of problem can be overcome by including consumption among the items to be predicted by the model, but only at the expense of re-defining final demand in such a way that it relates largely to the export sector, thereby introducing similar conceptual problems to those discussed earlier in connection with the export base multiplier.

The use of input–output models as a forecasting device is further limited by the assumptions that are made about the technical coefficients in the model. Like the export base multiplier, these coefficients must be estimated outside the model for future situations. If it is assumed that they remain constant, the possibilities of technological innovation, changing economies of scale, and the chances that alternative inputs will be substituted in the production process, are implicitly excluded from the analysis. For these reasons, and because of the problems associated with the estimation of final demand, input–output models must be seen as a means of estimating short-term fluctuations in the economy rather than as a means of predicting long-run economic growth.

There are also a number of practical problems associated with the definition of industrial sectors and the collection of data which must be considered. Generally, the most reliable estimates will be obtained where industrial sectors are narrowly defined and their products are homogeneous. The problems of data collection are related largely to the cost of its acquisition. For this reason composite tables are often constructed in which the transactions of the most important local industries are obtained by field survey and the remainder of the inter-industry table is interpolated from national or regional tables. In these cases, of course, the results will also reflect the extent to which the estimated transactions represent the local situation.

3 General Criteria for Planning Studies

Four main conclusions for planning studies emerge from an examination of the two models of economic activities that have been used most frequently in empirical work at the urban and regional level. Firstly, export base multipliers and input–output analyses are intended principally for short-term studies as they are concerned largely with these kinds of inter-relationships within the economy. They largely ignore the effects of technological changes and long-term growth processes that become increasingly influential over time. If used in projections for periods greater than ten years, then, the results obtained must be viewed with considerable caution.

Secondly, the range of error involved in the process of estimation, even for short periods, using either of these models, is likely to be considerable. This reflects the lack of precision involved in the definitions used in the accounting systems that form the basis for data collection and the large fluctuations that occur in many of the variables from year to year or even month to month. The range of possible errors also stems from the assumptions made in the export base multiplier that exports can be predicted outside the model, and in input–output analysis that all or part of the final demand sector can be projected in this way. As both models are dependent on estimates obtained from sources which lie outside the model itself, the additional assumptions made for this purpose will require careful scrutiny.

Thirdly, further increases in the range of error can be expected as the size of the area that is under consideration declines. As the number of establishments involved declines models of this kind are liable to become increasingly sensitive and vulnerable to large fluctuations, and the opening or closure of a single establishment may profoundly affect the projected levels of activity. The advantages related to the definition of the export base sector as the size of the area declines, are also offset to a large extent by the increasing importance that the definition of the area itself plays in these studies, and, in addition, projections for these areas tend to be increasingly dependent on factors outside the area, not merely in terms of the external trade estimates that form the base of the prediction, but also in the sense that decisions about local industries are largely taken outside the area itself by regional or national firms.

Lastly, there is the question of data collection for economic analyses of regions and urban areas. Regional accounting matrices and inter-industry input–output tables are highly complex systems which impose considerable strains on the resources that are generally available for data collection. In practice data of this kind are only occasionally available for areas less than the nation as a whole and tend to be assembled only for *ad hoc* regional studies and areas whose special features command this kind of treatment. Consequently, empirical work with these models must be viewed in terms of the limitations of the information that is available for this purpose. These limitations will affect not only the treatment of data within the model itself, but also the basic analysis of local economic structure which precedes the construction of the model.

Further Reading

Meyer's authoritative and wide ranging survey of regional economics (1963) is a useful starting point for further study which also contains an extensive bibliography. It summarises most of the topics that are dealt with in technical terms in Isard's massive textbook on methods of regional analysis (1960). Isard's work remains, however, the standard work of reference in the field, although Boudeville (1966, pp 75–101) deals more comprehensively with regional economic planning and Chapin (1965a, pp 107–180) describes some rule of thumb methods used in land use planning.

The elements of national income can be found in most textbooks on economics such as Samuelson (1969, pp 169–190) and Lipsey (1971, pp 438–453). A basic introduction to national income and social accounting is contained in Edey (1967) and the relationships between social accounting and economic models are described in Stone and Croft Murray's brief book (1959). Stone (1961) has also discussed accounting systems at the regional level in a useful review paper, while Leven (1961) describes some of the problems that are associated with the construction of regional income and product accounts.

Most works on input–output analysis contain an explanation of the methods used in the preparation of input–output tables. Yan (1969, pp 47–63) has an informative chapter explaining the concepts underlying the 1958 table for the United States economy. A more extended discussion of the methods used by various countries is contained in the United Nations review (1966) while the Central Statistical Office (1970) has produced a detailed explanation of the principles underlying tables summarised in table 3.3. The models and their limitations are discussed in general works such as Isard (1960, pp 335–343 and 363–371) as well as in the specialist literature. Regional input–output problems and the range of simplified models that have been devised to solve inter-regional problems are described fully by Yan (1969, pp 103–123) and also by Miernyck (1967, pp 58–77).

The state of the art in relation to the export base multiplier is reviewed in a useful paper by Lane (1966) which presents a balanced discussion of both the main approaches to empirical work. The main references have been gathered together by Pfouts (1960) in the form of a reader on urban economic analysis which presents the case for and against the use of the export (economic) base multiplier concept. In addition to these general references, potential workers in this field should consult Tiebout's (1962) valuable manual on base studies which illustrates the various degrees of refinement that can be attained in

F

empirical work. This book also describes the minimum requirements approach developed by Ulman and Dacey (1960).

Because of the difficulties involved in the use of the export base multiplier and input–output analysis for urban and regional economic analysis it is useful to consider some alternative methods that may, in some instances, be suitable for planning studies. Most of these methods, together with export base multipliers and input–output analysis, are comprehensively described by Isard (1960). Perhaps the most interesting of these methods from the point of view of urban and regional planners are industrial complex analysis and inter-regional linear programming. Industrial complex analysis is concerned with inter-industry transactions within an industrial complex of related activities, rather than in terms of the economy as a whole. It involves a more detailed examination of the comparative costs of production in terms of classical location theory than is the case in general studies. Inter-regional linear programming makes use of the mathematical programming techniques that have been developed to solve certain problems in operations research. It seeks to maximise or minimise some linear function subject to certain constraints. Typical functions in this case might include maximising regional income or minimising transportation costs.

A useful variant of the comparative cost approach has also been developed by Perloff, Dunn, Lampard, and Muth in their empirical work on the regions of the United States, entitled *Regions, Resources and Economic Growth* (1960). Termed shift share analysis, this method, in its simplest form, is concerned with the distinction between that proportion of regional growth which is associated with its shares of industries that are expanding or contracting nationally, and the changes within the industries themselves that shift in favour or against a region and give rise to regional growth rates which are higher or lower than the national average for that industry.

Another alternative which might meet certain of the requirements of urban and regional planners would involve the regionalisation of the models that are used for national economic forecasting purposes such as the short-term quarterly forecasting model constructed by the Brookings Institution for the United States as a whole (Duesenberry *et al*, 1964), or the medium-term model of economic growth constructed by the Department of Applied Economics at the University of Cambridge in Britain (Stone and Brown, 1962). However, considerable theoretical as well as practical obstacles must be overcome in this respect before models of this kind can be seen as anything other than a source for external estimates to regional and local studies (Klein, 1968). In the meantime, examples such as Czamanski's econometric forecasting model of the economy of Nova Scotia (1969), seem likely to remain exceptions to the general rule.

4. Spatial Organisation

The spatial organisation of population and economic activity within regions and urban areas influences planning in a very different way to studies of their overall structure and growth. It lies close to the heart of the planning process in that most decisions depend in some degree upon assumptions that have been made about the factors governing the locational choice of households, institutions, or businesses. They must take account not only of the spatial relationships surrounding each decision-making unit but also the extent to which individual choices are restricted by competition from other activities, and the amount of inertia in the system as a whole.

These choices underlie the whole city building process and its spatial organisation. They are reflected in the structure of the market for urban land which governs the prices that are paid for sites in each part of an urban area. They are also expressed in a number of interactions which are of special interest to planners. The distinction between the place of residence and the place of work, for instance, is of particular importance because of its implications on the demand for transportation at peak hours. Similarly, variations in the distribution of the residences of children of school age are likely to have a profound effect on educational provision, and differences in the distribution of potential consumers will largely govern the location of shopping or recreation facilities.

Urban and regional planners are mainly concerned with three aspects of spatial organisation. Firstly, they are interested in the factors governing the patterns of location of particular types of activity within a limited area. In the case of shopping they must consider how shopping activities are distributed throughout the study area and the extent to which changes in the overall pattern are influenced, on the one hand, by developments in the structure of retailing, and, on the other, by variations in shopping behaviour on the part of the consumer. Secondly, planners are concerned with the flows between different parts of the study area and the ways in which consumers respond to alterations in the transportation facilities that are available. Finally, local studies must interpret these locational patterns and flows of people and goods in terms of their effect on the environment of a limited part of the study area. In the process, they must translate their findings into the buildings and channels of communication which are the physical expression of the mixture of land uses within this area and, at the same time, seek ways by which they can guide future development towards the broad economic and social goals that have been defined by local residents.

The models that have been developed by urban and regional planners to analyse the spatial organisation of population and economic activity reflect most of these requirements. They express, in spatial terms, the basic elements that were described in the two preceding sections, and they are constructed in such a way that spatial relationships can be examined from different points of view with varying degrees of detail. Most of these models deal with spatial interaction at a particular point in time rather than as a dynamic process, but nevertheless they can be used to a limited extent to investigate the consequences of externally derived estimates of changes in population or economic activity on the spatial organisation of a region or urban area.

In the following section, only the elements of spatial interaction are described, and the discussion of analytical models deals exclusively with the gravity models that have been developed from an analogy between spatial relationships in urban and regional systems and Newton's law of gravity. Alternative forms of interaction model such as the intervening opportunities model and models of spatial organisation which do not represent interaction explicitly are listed in the final part of the chapter on further reading.

Basic Elements

The basic elements of population and economic activity have already been discussed in the two preceding chapters. In this part it is necessary only to describe the basic elements of the interaction matrix that is used for the analysis of spatial relationships, and to illustrate these by reference to a numerical example relating to journey to work flows in a large urban region.

TABLE 4.1

Some types of spatial interaction

Producer	Spatial relationship	Attractor
Workers' residences	Work trip distribution	Workplaces
Children's residences	School trip distribution	Schools
Shoppers' residences	Shopping trip distribution	Shops
Residential units' expenditure on retail goods	Shopping expenditure distribution	Retail sales
Recreators' residences	Recreation trip distribution	Recreation facilities
Residential units' expenditure on recreation	Recreation expenditure distribution	Recreation turnover
Manufacturing units⎫ Wholesaling units ⎬ Shopping units ⎭	Goods traffic distribution	⎧Manufacturing units ⎨Wholesaling units ⎩Shopping units

Spatial relationships are described by means of an interaction matrix which resembles in some ways the accounting matrix that was described in Chapter 3. Whereas the accounting matrix recorded transactions between buyers and sellers and distinguished between intermediate and final demand, the interaction matrix is used to record various types of activity involving producers and attractors. Some of these are expressed in terms of the trips that are made between two points within an urban area or region while others record cash transactions at shopping centres in terms of the place of residence of the shoppers.

Some of the main types of interaction matrix are illustrated in table 4.1 which also lists the producers and attractors in each case. In matrices of this type producers and attractors are defined in terms of the type of interaction that takes place between them. In a work trip analysis, for instance, producers and attractors will be defined as the number of workers living in each zone and the number of workers employed in each zone respectively. Similarly, for studies of shopping expenditure, producers will be measured by the level of household expenditure on retail goods and attractors by the sales at each shopping centre.

Generally, the term producer refers to the origin of a trip and the term attractor refers to its destination. For this reason, residential areas are usually viewed as producers or generators of demand which are satisfied at workplaces, schools, shops or places of entertainment. However no general distinction can be made between producers and attractors, for as the last entries in the table show, in some cases, the same activities act both as producers and attractors.

The form of the interaction matrix and the basic elements that it contains is as shown on the next page.

The interactions between each spatial unit or zone of producers and each of the attractors zones are recorded in the cells of this matrix. The entry in a_{11} records the intensity of interaction between producers in zone 1 and attractors in zone 1. In terms of the first kind of interaction that is listed in table 4.1 it would refer to the number of workers who live as well as work in zone 1. Similarly, an entry in a_{12} records the number of producers from zone 1 who have been attracted to zone 2. In terms of work trips, then, it would refer to the number of work trips made to workplaces in zone 2 by residents of zone 1. Conversely an entry in a_{21} records the number of producers in zone 2 who have been attracted to zone 1, or the number of work trips made by residents in zone 2 to workplaces in zone 1 in the case of work trips.

From \ To			Attractors			External zones	Total interaction produced
			Spatial units in study area				
			Zone 1	Zone 2	Zone 3		
Producers	Spatial units in study area	Zone 1	a_{11}	a_{12}	a_{13}	a_{14}	$\sum_j a_{1j}$
		Zone 2	a_{21}	a_{22}	a_{23}	a_{24}	$\sum_j a_{2j}$
		Zone 3	a_{31}	a_{32}	a_{33}	a_{34}	$\sum_j a_{3j}$
		Zone 4	a_{41}	a_{42}	a_{43}	a_{44}	$\sum_j a_{4j}$
		Zone 5	a_{51}	a_{52}	a_{53}	a_{54}	$\sum_j a_{5j}$
	External zones		a_{61}	a_{62}	a_{63}	0	$\sum_j a_{6j}$
Total interaction attracted			$\sum_i a_{i1}$	$\sum_i a_{i2}$	$\sum_i a_{i3}$	$\sum_i a_{i4}$	$\sum_i \sum_j a_{ij}$

The matrix as a whole shows the way in which the total amount of interaction that is produced by each zone is distributed between attractors, and also the way in which the total amount of interaction that is attracted by each zone is distributed between producers. For this reason it is often called a distribution matrix.

Two other features of the basic interaction matrix require further attention. Firstly, there may be differences between the spatial units used for producers and attractors. In the case of work trips, for example, the production zones may be defined in terms of residential areas while the attraction zones are defined in terms of workplaces. However, where more complex sets of interactions are involved, and where most of the spatial units contain a mixture of activities, it is generally desirable to keep some measure of consistency in the definition of zone systems. Secondly, in all studies of this kind provision should be made for the recording of interactions that cross the boundaries of the area that is under consideration. In some situations, such as the case of a large regional shopping centre, these interactions may be of considerable importance and further subdivision of these external interactions may be necessary.

Table 4.1 also gives some indication of the varying degrees of complexity that are involved in the analysis of spatial interaction. Work trips and school trips present relatively few problems as they involve regular trips by easily identifiable producers between well defined points. Shopping and recreational trips, however, present a much more complex pattern of spatial relationships. These trips are much more varied in nature and also less regular in terms of the individuals concerned. Producers are more difficult to define for nearly everyone at some point in time can be considered as a potential producer of trips to certain types of shop or particular kinds of recreation facility. Furthermore, it is also necessary to consider these patterns in terms of overall travel behaviour as many shopping or recreation trips take place in the context of another trip. For instance, a worker may travel each day from home to work, do some shopping in his lunch break, and then visit friends on his way home. In cases of this kind the location of these secondary activities is dependent not only on the location of the producer's residence, but also other attractors.

The general principles underlying the use of interaction matrices are illustrated in table 4.2 which shows the journey to work flows that were recorded for the Merseyside area in the 1966 ten per cent sample census. In this case 64 275(0) work trips were produced from places of residence in the study area and 66 048(0) work trips were attracted to places of employment in this area. The vast majority of work trips started from places of residence and ended at places of employment which were located within the study area, but 3835(0) residents travelled to work outside Merseyside and 5608(0) employees travelled to Merseyside from residences in other areas.

The ways in which the table describes the distribution of work trips can be seen from an examination of the first row and the first column of this table which refer to Bootle. At the time of the census 3538(0)

TABLE 4.2

Journey to work flows on Merseyside 1966

From	To	Zones North of River Mersey							
		Bootle CB	Crosby MB	Huyton UD	Kirkby UD	Litherland UD	Liverpool CB*	Liverpool central area	W
Zones North of River Mersey	Bootle CB	1785	103		48	115	845	399	
	Crosby MB	343	866		25	101	448	514	
	Huyton UD	37		667	166		1054	509	
	Kirkby UD	80	7	5	1216		577	247	
	Litherland UD	272	122		12	283	225	181	
	Liverpool CB*	989	79	210	819	33	18 494	7428	
	Liverpool central area	10					94	258	
	Whiston RD	21		84	114		669	284	
Zones South of River Mersey	Bebington MB	9					71	273	
	Birkenhead CB	24					213	773	
	Ellesmere Port MB						11	18	
	Hoylake UD						113	337	
	Neston UD						29	66	
	Wallasey CB	40			14		262	872	
	Wirral UD						90	255	
	Total	3610	1177	966	2414	532	23 195	12 414	
	Work trips produced by external zones	372	130	98	342	45	1478	1426	
	Total work trips attracted to study area	3982	1307	1064	2756	577	24 673	13 840	

Source: Sample Census 1966 Workplace and Transport Tables part 1, tables 2, 3, and 4.
Note: External trips also include some trips within the study area that are not tabulated separately in the published tables.
* Liverpool CB excludes the central area which is treated as a separate zone in this table.

	Zones South of River Mersey							Work trips attracted by external zones	Total work trips produced in study area
ion	*Birkenhead CB*	*Ellesmere Port MB*	*Hoylake UD*	*Neston UD*	*Wallasey CB*	*Wirral UD*	*Total*		
	24	7					3375	163	3538
	17				6		2334	162	2496
	22	5					2601	326	2927
	14	6					2169	109	2278
	5						1116	56	1172
	308	91			60		29 263	1124	30 387
	6						368	27	395
	8						1848	980	2828
	339	246		16	16	14	2320	113	2433
	3469	292	29	13	256	75	6012	185	6197
	25	1914		6	6	10	2080	236	2316
	148	26	507	5	72	11	1270	72	1342
	44	51		266	5	8	517	92	609
	782	113	67	9	1810	16	4125	137	4262
	203	41	18	19	24	341	1042	53	1095
	5414	2792	621	334	2255	475	60 440	3835	64 275
	113	583	30	17	29	15	5608		
	5527	3375	651	351	2284	490	66 048		

work trips were produced by residents of Bootle. Nearly half of these (1785(0)) involved journeys to places of employment which were in the same area, while most of the remainder travelled to Liverpool and its central area to work. Conversely 3982(0) trips were attracted to work-places in Bootle. As before, 1785(0) of these were local trips which were also produced in Bootle, and most of the remainder came from Liverpool, but substantial flows were also recorded from Crosby, Litherland, and external zones. When these two distributions are compared it can be seen that there was a net inflow of workers to Bootle from Crosby, Litherland, and the external zones, while there was a net outflow to Liverpool and its central area as a whole.

The table also shows the general pattern of commuting within the urban region. In this case, the region is dominated by Liverpool which accounted for nearly half the total number of work trips produced, and if its central area is included, for nearly three-fifths of the total number of trips attracted in 1966. Because Liverpool and its central area are a net attractor of work trips there are considerable differences between the distribution of trips produced and trips attracted to the city. Seven-eighths of the trips produced in Liverpool are attracted to destinations in the city whereas only two-thirds of the trips attracted to Liverpool are produced in the city. Consequently there is a net inflow of workers to places of employment in Liverpool from all parts of the urban region.

The extent to which the river Mersey inhibits interaction between its north and south banks can also be estimated from this table. Apart from the flows to Liverpool and its central area in particular from the south bank, and some reverse flows from the north bank to Birkenhead, there is very little cross-river commuting on Merseyside and the urban region can be divided into two distinct parts for the analysis of work trips.

An examination of the pattern and distribution of external trips gives some indication of the extent to which the area that is under considera-tion can be treated as a distinct labour market area from the viewpoint of the journey to work. In this case, it can be seen that, although the total number of external trips is small by comparison with internal trips, it was very unevenly distributed between different parts of the study area. It constitutes a considerable proportion of the total number of trips that were produced and attracted to some zones like Huyton, Whiston, or Ellesmere Port which are located on the edges of the study area. In Whiston, for example, over a third of all work trips crossed the boundary. Consequently, while the area as a whole can be viewed as a distinct labour market area, some flexibility is required in interpreting this conclusion in terms of its internal spatial structure.

Analytical Models

The most frequently used models for analysing spatial relationships in regions and urban areas are interaction models which were initially derived from the analogy relating spatial interaction to Newton's law of gravitational force. Newton's law states that the gravitational force between two masses is a function of the product of the masses themselves and inversely proportional to the distance between them. In interaction models, the strength of gravitational force is usually measured in terms of the intensity of interaction between different zones which can be estimated by reference to the masses that produce or attract this interaction and the distance separating them.

Models of this kind have been used in a variety of ways in the analysis of spatial organisation, and an alternative form of model termed the intervening opportunities model has also been developed, which assumes that the intensity of interaction is inversely proportional to the number of intervening opportunities between two masses rather than the distance between them. Apart from this difference, however, the intervening opportunities model can be developed in the same way as the gravity model. Consequently, the following part deals only with the types of model that have been derived from the basic analogy with Newton's law of gravity, and the composite models that have been devised which link together some of these types. It also describes, in general terms, the way in which these models can be reformulated statistically by means of an entropy maximising methodology, and concludes with a discussion of the principles underlying the use of these models in planning studies.

1 *The Family of Gravity Models*

The simplest form of gravity model is derived directly from the Newtonian analogy. This states that the intensity of interaction (G_{ij}) between area i and area j is a function of the relative attractiveness of each area $(W_i$ and $W_j)$ and that it is inversely proportional to some function of the distance between them (d_{ij}):

$$G_{ij} = KW_iW_j\, d_{ij}^{-\alpha} \qquad (4.1)$$

where K and α are predetermined constants.

If K was equal to $0{\cdot}5$, and the values of W_i and W_j were 10 and 20 respectively in a situation where the distance between them was 2 miles and the constant α was 2, the volume of interaction between them estimated by the model would be 25 (ie, $0{\cdot}5 \times 10 \times 20 \times 1/(2 \times 2)$).

The interaction models that are generally used in planning studies incorporate certain refinements to this basic model which initially arose out of experience gained in its use in transport studies. These studies are primarily concerned with interaction in terms of the distribution of a given number of trips produced by a particular zone in relation to competing centres of attraction. In these models the number of trips produced or attracted by each zone can be used as the mass variables instead of the measures of relative attractiveness described above. For this reason certain constraints must be introduced to ensure that there is internal consistency within the model between the estimated distribution of trips and the externally derived trip totals that are used to derive these estimates. As the number of constraints used varies according to the inclusion or omission of external estimates of the numbers of trips produced and attracted it is possible to distinguish four different kinds of gravity model. These are the modified version of the unconstrained model described above, a production and attraction constrained model, a production constrained model, and an attraction constrained model shown below:

Estimates required prior to calculation

	Modified unconstrained model	Production and attraction constrained model	Production constrained model	Attraction constrained model
Distance (d_{ij})	Yes	Yes	Yes	Yes
Constant (α)	Yes	Yes	Yes	Yes
Number of trips:				
Produced (O_i)	Yes	Yes	Yes	No
Attracted (D_j)	Yes	Yes	No	Yes
Generalised measures of attraction:				
Produced (W_i)	No	No	No	Yes
Attracted (W_j)	No	No	Yes	No

The unconstrained model described above can be revised to express interaction in terms of an exogenous or externally derived estimate of the total number of trips in the system as a whole. With reference to the distribution of work trips, this is achieved in the following way:

$$T_{ij} = KO_i D_j d_{ij}^{-\alpha} \qquad (4.2)$$

where T_{ij} is the number of trips made by residents in zone i to work in zone j

$\quad O_i$ is the number of workers living in zone i

$\quad D_j$ is the number of jobs in zone j

$\quad d_{ij}$ is the distance between zone i and zone j

$\quad \alpha$ is a predetermined constant

and

$$K = \frac{\sum_i O_i}{\sum_i \sum_j T_{ij}} = \frac{\sum_j D_j}{\sum_i \sum_j T_{ij}}$$

In this case the general measures of zonal attractiveness (W_i, W_j) are replaced by measures of the numbers of trips produced (O_i) and attracted (D_j), and K is determined within the model instead of being predetermined as in the previous equation. The constant K now represents the scaling factor that is required to express estimates of total interaction of the kind derived from the previous equation as estimates which will add up to the total number of work trips in the system.

The manner in which this model operates and further refinements to the model as a whole can be illustrated by reference to a simple example involving three zones and 1000 work trips:

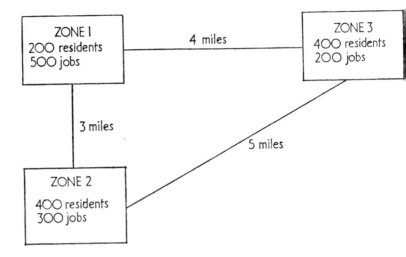

In this case the average distance travelled within each zone from home to work is assumed to be two miles and α is given the predetermined value of 2.

The total interaction between all zones must be estimated before the value of the constant K can be calculated for this system. This is derived by multiplying out the basic equation for each pair of zones between which interaction takes place, giving K the value of 1. For instance, the interaction between residents in zone 1 and jobs in zone 1 will be 25 000 (ie, $1 \times 200 \times 500 \times 1/(2 \times 2)$), while that between residents in zone 1 and jobs in zone 2 is 6667 (ie, $1 \times 200 \times 300 \times 1/(3 \times 3)$). Similarly, the interaction between residents in zone 2 and jobs in zone 1 will be 22 222 (ie, $1 \times 400 \times 500 \times 1/(3 \times 3)$), and 12 500 for residents in zone 3 and jobs in zone 1 (ie, $1 \times 400 \times 500 \times 1/(4 \times 4)$).

In this way a matrix of interactions can be constructed which can be used to calculate the total amount of interaction in the system as a whole:

		Jobs			Total residents
	Zone	1	2	3	
Residents	1	25 000	6667	2500	34 167
	2	22 222	30 000	3200	55 422
	3	12 500	4800	20 000	37 300
Total Jobs		59 722	41 467	25 700	126 889

From this matrix it can be seen that the total interaction predicted in the model is 126 889. This volume of interaction must now be adjusted so that it is made equivalent to the total number of trips given at the start of the exercise in terms of this example, which refers to 1000 work trips, then, the value of the scaling factor K that is required for this purpose will be 0·007 881 (ie, 1000/126 889). If each of the estimates of interaction shown above are multiplied by this factor a trip distribution matrix will be estimated.

G

		Jobs			Estimated residents
	Zone	1	2	3	
	1	197	52	20	269
Residents	2	175	236	25	436
	3	99	38	158	295
Estimated Jobs		471	326	203	1000

The only constraint imposed on this model was that implicit in the estimation of the constant K which was that the total number of work trips in the system as a whole should be 1000. As no further constraints were included in the model there are substantial discrepancies between the total number of residents and jobs predicted from the trip distribution and those used to generate this distribution (the O_i's and D_j's). For instance, 269 residents and 471 jobs are allocated to zone 1 by the model whereas only 200 residents and 500 jobs were allocated to this zone in the externally derived estimates. Similarly 436 residents and 326 jobs are allocated to zone 2 as against 400 residents and 300 jobs in the initial estimates and only 295 residents and 203 jobs are allocated to zone 3 by the model as against 400 residents and 200 jobs in the initial estimates.

A more sophisticated constraints procedure is required to ensure that the estimated distribution of jobs and residents in each zone is the same as that given in the initial estimates. It involves two separate sets of scaling factors which must be estimated for each zone. This production and attraction constrained model can be expressed as follows using the notation defined for the preceding equation:

$$T_{ij} = A_i B_j O_i D_j d_{ij}^{-\alpha} \tag{4.3}$$

where

$$A_i = 1/\sum_j B_j D_j d_{ij}^{-\alpha} \tag{4.4}$$

$$B_j = 1/\sum_i A_i O_i d_{ij}^{-\alpha} \tag{4.5}$$

and there are two sets of constraints:

$$\sum_i T_{ij} = D_j$$

$$\sum_j T_{ij} = O_i$$

As the basic equation (4.3) in this model contains two sets of unknowns in the scaling factors A_i and B_j, each of which can only be solved by calculating the value of the other, it is necessary to estimate the values involved iteratively within the two minor equations (4.4 and 4.5). This procedure requires that arbitrary values for either A_i or B_j are used initially to enable the other scaling factors to be calculated. Once these are calculated they can be used to recalculate the initial scaling factors until the difference between the values predicted at each round of calculations, or iterations, is considered to be unimportant. Given estimates for the scaling factors calculated in this way, eq (4.3) can be solved to estimate the distribution of trips.

The solution of the production and attraction constrained gravity model and the process of iteration that is used for this purpose can be illustrated in relation to the three-zone example. Assuming an initial value of 1 for each B_j, the calculations required for the first two iterations are given in table 4.3.

Three separate steps are involved in each estimation of each of the scaling factors. Firstly, taking the example of the calculation of A_i for zone 1 using eq (4.4), it is necessary to estimate for each set of inter-actions the values of $B_j D_j d_{ij}^{-\alpha}$. Secondly, the results of these estimates must be summed up, and thirdly, the value of A_i will be found by taking the reciprocal of the summed estimates. For zone 1, then, B_1, B_2, and B_3 are all assumed to be 1, the values of $B_j D_j d_{ij}^{-2}$ for each of the three destination zones will be 125 (ie, $1 \times 500 \times 1/(2 \times 2)$) for jobs in zone 1, 33·3 (ie, $1 \times 300 \times 1/(3 \times 3)$) for jobs in zone 2, and 12·5 (ie, $1 \times 200 \times 1/(4 \times 4)$) for jobs in zone 3. The sum of these values ($\sum_j B_j D_j d_{ij}^{-2}$) will be 170·8 and the reciprocal of this sum ($1/\sum_j B_j D_j d_{ij}^{-2}$) or A_i will be 0·00585 (ie, 1/170·8). Similarly the initial values of A_i for zones 2 and 3 can be calculated as 0·007 22 and 0·01072 respectively from the table.

Given these values of A_i, a new cycle of calculations can begin with the re-estimation of each B_j using eq (4.5). The process outlined above

TABLE 4.3

Production and attraction constrained gravity model worked example

FIRST ITERATION

Estimation of A_i (eq. (4.4))

	Residents in zone 1 $B_J D_J d_{iJ}^{-2}$	Residents in zone 2 $B_J D_J d_{iJ}^{-2}$	Residents in zone 3
Jobs zone 1	$1 \times 500 \times 1/(2 \times 2) = 125$	$1 \times 500 \times 1/(3 \times 3) = 55 \cdot 6$	$31 \cdot 25$
Jobs zone 2	$1 \times 300 \times 1/(3 \times 3) = 33 \cdot 3$	$1 \times 300 \times 1/(2 \times 2) = 75$	12
Jobs zone 3	$1 \times 200 \times 1/(4 \times 4) = 12 \cdot 5$	$1 \times 200 \times 1/(5 \times 5) = 8$	50
$\sum_J B_J D_J d_{iJ}^{-2}$	$170 \cdot 8$	$138 \cdot 6$	$93 \cdot 25$
$A_i = 1/\sum_J B_J D_J d_{iJ}^{-2}$	$0 \cdot 005\ 85$	$0 \cdot 007\ 22$	$0 \cdot 010\ 72$

Estimation of B_j (eq. (4.5))

	Jobs in zone 1 $A_i O_i d_{iJ}^{-2}$	Jobs in zone 2 $A_i O_i d_{iJ}^{-2}$	Jobs in zone 3
Res. zone 1	$0 \cdot 005\ 85 \times 200 \times 1/(2 \times 2) = 0 \cdot 2925$	$0 \cdot 005\ 85 \times 200 \times 1/(3 \times 3) = 0 \cdot 1300$	$0 \cdot 0731$
Res. zone 2	$0 \cdot 007\ 22 \times 400 \times 1/(3 \times 3) = 0 \cdot 3209$	$0 \cdot 007\ 22 \times 400 \times 1/(2 \times 2) = 0 \cdot 7220$	$0 \cdot 1155$
Res. zone 3	$0 \cdot 010\ 72 \times 400 \times 1/(4 \times 4) = 0 \cdot 2675$	$0 \cdot 010\ 72 \times 400 \times 1/(5 \times 5) = 0 \cdot 1715$	$1 \cdot 0720$
$\sum_i A_i O_i d_{iJ}^{-2}$	$0 \cdot 8809$	$1 \cdot 0235$	$1 \cdot 2606$
$B_J = 1/\sum_i A_i O_i d_{iJ}^{-2}$	$1 \cdot 135$	$0 \cdot 9770$	$0 \cdot 7932$

SECOND ITERATION

Examination of A_i (eq (4.4))

	Residents in zone 1 $B_j D_j d_{ij}^{-2}$	Residents in zone 2 $B_j D_j d_{ij}^{-2}$	Residents in zone 3 $B_j D_j d_{ij}^{-2}$
Jobs zone 1	$1\cdot135 \times 500 \times 1/(2 \times 2) = 141\cdot9$	$1\cdot135 \times 500 \times 1/(3 \times 3) = 63\cdot1$	35·5
Jobs zone 2	$0\cdot9700 \times 300 \times 1/(3 \times 3) = 325$	$0\cdot9770 \times 300 \times 1/(2 \times 2) = 73\cdot3$	11·7
Jobs zone 3	$0\cdot7932 \times 200 \times 1/(4 \times 4) = 9\cdot9$	$0\cdot7932 \times 200 \times 1/(5 \times 5) = 6\cdot3$	39·7
$\sum_i B_j D_j d_{ij}^{-2}$	184·3	142·7	86·9
$A_i = 1/\sum_j B_j D_j d_{ij}^{-2}$	0·005 43	0·007 01	0·011 51

Estimation of B_j (eq. 4.5)

	Jobs in zone 1 $A_i O_i d_{ij}^{-2}$	Jobs in zone 2 $A_i O_i d_{ij}^{-2}$	Jobs in zone 3 $A_i O_i d_{ij}^{-2}$
Res. zone 1	$0\cdot005\ 43 \times 200 \times 1/(2 \times 2) = 0\cdot2715$	$0\cdot005\ 43 \times 200 \times 1/(3 \times 3) = 0\cdot1207$	0·0679
Res. zone 2	$0\cdot007\ 01 \times 400 \times 1/(3 \times 3) = 0\cdot3116$	$0\cdot007\ 01 \times 400 \times 1/(2 \times 2) = 0\cdot7010$	0·1122
Res. zone 3	$0\cdot011\ 51 \times 400 \times 1/(4 \times 4) = 0\cdot2878$	$0\cdot011\ 51 \times 400 \times 1/(5 \times 5) = 0\cdot1842$	1·1510
$\sum_i A_i O_i d_{ij}^{-2}$	0·8709	1·0059	1·3311
$B_j = 1/\sum_i A_i O_i d_{ij}^{-2}$	1·1482	0·9941	0·7512

is repeated for each of the three zones giving values of 1·135, 0·9700, and 0·7932 for each of the respective B_j's. Having obtained these values a further cycle of calculations can be undertaken in respect of the estimation of the values of A_i using eq (4.4), which in turn will generate further estimates of B_j using eq (4.5). With each iteration the difference between the values calculated and those calculated in the previous iteration will diminish and the system will be said to converge when a predetermined reduction in differences is reached. In this case five iterations are required for a reduction in all the differences of less than 0·001.

| | *Iteration Number:* | | | | |
	1	2	3	4	5
A_1	0·005 85	0·005 43	0·005 37	0·005 37	0·005 36
A_2	0·007 22	0·007 01	0·006 93	0·006 90	0·006 90
A_3	0·010 72	0·011 52	0·011 72	0·011 77	0·011 78
B_1	1·134 37	1·148 33	1·150 14	1·150 46	1·150 54
B_2	0·977 14	0·994 15	1·000 44	1·002 20	1·002 66
B_3	0·793 00	0·750 90	0·741 00	0·738 54	0·737 91

The values of A_i and B_j that were obtained in the last iteration can now be used to estimate the number of trips between each pair of zones using eq (4.3).

As a result of the use of the more complex constraints procedure in this model the values of the sums of the distributed trips in terms of both residents and jobs is the same as the initial estimates of the number of trips produced by and attracted to each zone. When compared with the trip distribution predicted by the crude model as formulated in eq (4.2), it will be noted that there are substantial differences in the volumes of

		Jobs			Total residents
	Zone	1	2	3	
	1	154	36	10	200
Residents	2	176	208	16	400
	3	169	57	174	400
Total Jobs		500	300	200	1000

(Note: numbers in this and subsequent tables may not add up precisely because of rounding.)

interaction predicted for some zones. For instance, 169 trips by residents of zone 3 to work in zone 1 are predicted by the more complex model as against 99 trips predicted by the crude model.

Not all gravity models have both the productions and attractions specified in this way. In many cases, while the production or the attraction is defined in these terms, the other variable is expressed by general measures of a zonal attractiveness of the kind used in the unconstrained model shown in eq (4.1). The solution of the two versions of the model produced by these means is much simpler than that used in the production and attraction constrained model as only one constraint must be satisfied in each case. The production constrained model, in which the home ends of the home based trips (O_i) are given in the external estimates, takes the following form in the notation used earlier:

$$T_{ij} = A_i O_i W_j d_{ij}^{-\alpha} \qquad (4.6)$$

where
$$A_i = 1/\sum_j W_j d_{ij}^{-\alpha} \qquad (4.7)$$

and there is only one constraint:

$$\sum_j T_{ij} = O$$

The attraction constrained model, in which the non-home ends of the home based trips (D_j) are given in the external estimates, takes the following form in the same notation:

$$T_{ij} = B_j D_j W_i d_{ij}^{-\alpha} \tag{4.8}$$

where $$B_j = 1/\sum_i W_i d_{ij}^{-\alpha} \tag{4.9}$$

and there is only one constraint:

$$\sum_i T_{ij} = D_j$$

The solution of both these versions of the gravity model can be illustrated by further reference to the three-zone example. In the case of the production constrained model measures of the relative attractiveness of the attractors (W_j's) are required in addition to the information given above. If W_1 is 60, W_2 is 90, and W_3 is 80 then the value of each A_i can be found using eq (4.7) by the three-stage calculation described above. In the case of the first zone, the first step is to calculate $W_j d_{ij}^{-\alpha}$ for each of the interactions:

Attraction of zone 1 $\quad 60 \times 1/(2 \times 2) = 15$

Attraction of zone 2 $\quad 90 \times 1/(3 \times 3) = 10$

Attraction of zone 3 $\quad 80 \times 1/(4 \times 4) = 5$

The sum of these calculations ($\sum_j W_j d_{ij}^{-\alpha}$) will be 30, and consequently A_1 will be 0·0333 (ie, 1/30). Similarly, A_2 will be 0·0309 and A_3 will be 0·0366 in this case.

When these values are used in eq (4.6) to estimate the distribution of trips between zones, a matrix will be produced (see next page).

As a result of the constraints procedure used in this model the number of residents estimated will agree with the external estimates of producers (ie, $\sum_j T_{ij} = O_i$). On the other hand the measures of zonal attractiveness used in this model have enabled the number of jobs resulting from the trip distribution to be estimated on the basis of the weightings contained in these factors. Consequently, there is a basic difference between these results and those obtained by the production

	Jobs			Total residents
Zone	1	2	3	
Residents 1	100	67	33	200
Residents 2	82	278	40	400
Residents 3	55	53	292	400
Total Jobs	237	398	365	1000

and attraction constrained model which is of special importance for the analysis of interactions of the kind listed in table 4.1. Whereas the double constrained model can only be used to estimate the distribution of trips between zones, the production constrained model can also be used to estimate the number of trips that is attracted to each destination zone. It can be used, for instance, to calculate the number of shopping trips or the volume of trade that would be attracted to each shopping centre from predetermined estimates of the number of trips or the amount of expenditure generated by each residential zone. Similarly, the attraction constrained model can be used to estimate the residential population of each zone for predetermined estimates of the number of trips attracted by each destination zone. On this basis a number of useful models can be developed to explore the spatial consequences of interaction patterns in regions and urban areas.

These kinds of application can be illustrated by formulating the production constrained model so that it can be used to estimate the volume of retail sales in each shopping centre which is produced by given estimates of household expenditure. In this case interaction will be expressed in terms of the amount of money that is spent by residents of zone i at shopping centres in zone j, and eqs (4.6) and (4.7) will take the following form:

$$T_{ij} = A_i O_i W_j d_{ij}^{-\alpha} \tag{4.6}$$

where $\qquad A_i \quad = 1/\sum_j W_j d_{ij}^{-\alpha}$ (4.7)

and $\qquad \sum_j T_{ij} = O_i$

In this case, however,

T_{ij} is the amount of money spent by residents of zone i at shopping centres in zone j.

O_i is the amount of money spent by residents of zone i on all shopping goods.

W_j is some measure of the relative attractiveness of zone j as a shopping centre.

$d_{ij}^{-\alpha}$ is some function of the distance between zone i and zone j.

The use of this kind of model can be shown by further reference to the numerical example. Given that the values for productions, attractions and distances are the same as those used above, and that each producer spends £50 on retail goods, the following matrix will be estimated:

£

	Zone	Shopping centres			Total household expenditure
		1	2	3	
Household Expenditure	1	5000	3335	1665	10 000
	2	4120	13 905	1975	20 000
	3	2740	2635	14 625	20 000
Total retail sales		11 860	19 875	18 265	50 000

As a result of this table the total volume of retail sales at each shopping centre which is drawn from households in the study area can be calculated as £11 860 for the shopping centre in zone 1, and £19 875 and £18 265 respectively for the shopping centres in zone 2 and zone 3.

Models of this kind can also be used in several ways to explore the implications of changes in the distribution of producers on attractors and vice versa, as they give some indication of the kind of impact that these changes would have on spatial relationships as a whole if the general pattern of existing behaviour continued. In the example referred to above, for example, possible changes in household expenditure relating to certain zones could be examined in terms of their effect on the level of retail sales at each shopping centre. If, for instance, the volume of household expenditure in zone 1 increased by £10 000 from £10 000 to £20 000, it can easily be calculated that this would result in additional sales of £5000, £3335, and £1665 in each of the three shopping centres respectively.

Similar experiments can be carried out in relation to the effect that changes in the values of the attraction factors for each of these centres, or changes in the estimated distances between zones might have on the volume of expenditure at each of these shopping centres. At the same time models of this kind can be used to explore the implications of overall changes in behaviour in so far as they are expressed in the interaction matrix. By varying the value of α used in the distance function, for instance, the consequences of changes in the effect of distance upon expenditure patterns can be considered.

The effects of some of these possible variations can be seen from a table (on the next page).

The results of these variations on the total sales at each shopping centre show some interesting features. As might be expected, local shopping centres get the main advantage from the doubling of the household expenditure produced by zone 1, but zone 2 also benefits substantially because of its proximity to this zone by comparison with zone 3. However, the doubling of the attractive power of this zone results in only a 30 per cent increase in total sales over the initial estimate. In this case the relative proximity of zone 1 to zone 2 is reflected in a correspondingly greater proportional decline of sales at this centre as against the decline at zone 3.

The effect of halving the distance between zones 1 and 3 seems confusing at first sight. On the one hand zone 1's sales increase by

Variation type		Initial example	Change in producers Add. £10 000 to producers in zone 1	Change in attraction Add. 90 to attraction of zone 2	Change in network Distance between zone 1 and 3 halved	Change in behaviour $\alpha = 1\cdot5$
		£	£	£	£	£
	1	11 860	16 860	8600	15 225	12 360
Shopping centre	2	19 875	23 210	26 060	17 990	19 840
	3	18 265	19 930	15 340	16 785	17 800
Total sales		50 000	60 000	50 000	50 000	50 000

nearly 30 per cent over the initial estimate, while on the other, zone 3's sales decline as a result of having a larger volume of expenditure within easy reach. The explanation of this apparent anomaly lies in the size of the initial estimate of local household expenditure, which was £10 000 for zone 1 and £20 000 for zone 2. As a result of the change in distance the volume of local expenditure for both centres increases to £30 000, but in the case of zone 1 this represents a threefold increase whereas in zone 3 it gives rise to only a 50 per cent increase. Consequently, in spite of the fact that the reduction in distance is felt by both centres, it benefits zone 1 far more than zone 3.

The consequences of an overall change in shopping behaviour are reflected mainly in the distribution matrix and in the mean distance travelled rather than in the total volume of sales at each centre. A reduction in the value of α lessens the effects of distance on shopping behaviour. Consequently, there is a reduction in the volume of expenditure that is produced and consumed within the same zone. The main beneficiary from these changes is the zone which is the most accessible to all the other zones, and the main loser is the zone which is least accessible to all zones. For this reason zone 1 gains from a reduction in the value of α while zone 3 sales show a slight decline.

2 *The Lowry Model*

Under certain circumstances, the two kinds of single constraint gravity model can be linked together to form a composite model in which the output of one gravity model becomes the input to another. The best example of a composite model is the Lowry model which generates estimates of the distribution of population and service employment within a region or an urban area at a given point in time. It utilises both the production constrained gravity model and the attraction constrained gravity models that were described in the last section and the concept of the export base multiplier that was described in Chapter 3. (Lowry, 1964).

In its simplest form the Lowry model makes two basic assumptions about the factors governing the location of activities in regions and urban areas. Firstly, it is assumed that an individual's choice of residential location is strongly influenced by the location of his place of work. Secondly, it is assumed that economic activities can be divided into two categories on the basis of their locational requirements. They can be classified as basic activities where their location within the area is determined by factors outside the scope of the model, or as service activities where their location is seen to be largely a function of the distribution of population.

On the basis of these assumptions, the distribution of population and service employment can be predicted from a given distribution of basic employment by means of an iterative process. In this process the distribution of resident workers is first calculated from the distribution of basic employment by means of an attraction constrained gravity model. Then the estimates of resident workers are multiplied by the activity rate (as defined in section 3) to convert them into estimates of residential population. Given this estimate the destination of the service trips made by the residential population can be calculated by means of a production constrained gravity model, and converted into employment estimates by multiplying them by the ratio of service jobs to total population.

The second iteration begins using the distribution of service employment calculated in the first cycle as the input to the attraction constrained gravity model instead of the distribution of basic employment. This generates further distributions of residential population and service employment which form the input to the third iteration of the model. In this way a series of calculations is begun which is repeated until an equilibrium distribution is reached which is generally after four or five iterations. At this stage the total distribution of population and service employment can be calculated by adding up the zonal estimates from each iteration.

The general processes of calculation involved in the Lowry model can be described more precisely by a series of equations beginning with the attraction constrained gravity model which is used to find the distribution of the residences of the workers:

$$T_{ij} = B_j D_j W_i d_{ij}^{-\alpha} \tag{4.10}$$

where
$$B_j = 1/\sum_i W_i d_{ij}^{-\alpha} \tag{4.11}$$

and
$$\sum_i T_{ij} = D_j$$

In this case T_{ij} is the number of trips made by residents in zone i to work in zone j.

$\quad\quad D_j$ is the number of jobs in zone j. In the first iteration this will represent basic employment and in subsequent iterations it will represent progressively diminishing increments of service employment.

$\quad\quad W_i$ is some measure of the attractiveness of zone i as a residential location.

$\quad\quad d_{ij}^{-\alpha}$ is the distance between zone i and zone j, expressed in terms of the predetermined function α.

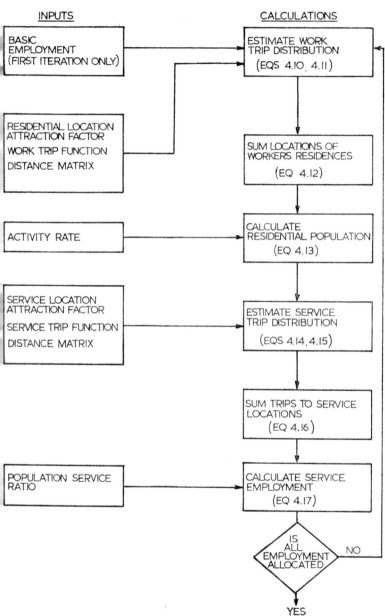

FIG. 2.   Flow diagram of the Lowry model

The number of resident workers living in zone i (C_i) can be calculated by summing up the distribution of trips:

$$C_i = \sum_j T_{ij} \tag{4.12}$$

This can be converted to resident population (O_i) by reference to an activity rate:

$$O_i = C_i \, 1/AR \tag{4.13}$$

where AR is the activity rate expressing total employment as a proportion of total population (ie, E_T/P).

From the distribution of residential population the distribution of service trips can be calculated by a production constrained gravity model:

$$T_{ij} = A_i O_i W_j d_{ij}^{-\alpha} \tag{4.14}$$

where

$$A_i = 1/\sum_j W_j d_{ij}^{-\alpha} \tag{4.15}$$

and

$$\sum_j T_{ij} = O_i$$

In this case T_{ij} is the number of service trips made by residents in zone i to services in zone j.

O_i is the residential population of zone i.

W_j is some measure of the attractiveness of zone j as a service centre.

$d_{ij}^{-\alpha}$ is the distance between zone i and zone j expressed in terms of a predetermined function α.

From this equation the total number of service trips made to zone j (S_j) can be calculated by summing up the distribution of trips

$$S_j = \sum_i T_{ij} \tag{4.16}$$

This figure can be converted to an estimate of service employment (D_{1j}) by reference to the population service ratio

$$D_{1j} = S_j \, PSR \tag{4.17}$$

where *PSR* is the ratio which expresses service employment as a proportion of the total population (ie, E_S/P).

This estimate of service employment forms the input to eq 4.10 in the first step of the second cycle of calculations.

The general principles underlying this model can be illustrated by a five-zone example for a region with a population of 5000 and a labour force of 2000 of whom half are employed in jobs classified as basic in terms of their location. The example concerns a seaport (zone 1) which is the location of the 1000 basic jobs in the region and four other zones representing areas for development at varying distances from the port.

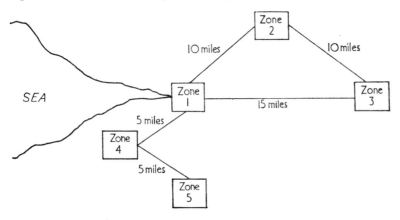

If it is assumed that the average distance travelled within each zone will be 2 miles, an interzonal distance matrix can be derived from this communications network (on next page).

The attractiveness of each of these zones for residential development in this example might be expressed by a measure of its land area:

Zone	Land area (square miles)
1	10
2	12
3	12
4	10
5	15

H

Miles

		To Zone:				
		1	2	3	4	5
From Zone:	1	2	10	15	5	10
	2	10	2	10	15	20
	3	15	10	2	20	25
	4	5	15	20	2	5
	5	10	20	25	5	2

The attractiveness of each of these zones for service employment in this example might be expressed by a measure of existing service floor space:

Zone	Floor space (*thousands square feet*)
1	5
2	2
3	1
4	10
5	2

The overall activity rate will be 0·40 (ie, 2000/5000) and the population service ratio 0·20 (ie, 1000/5000). With this information, together with the assumption that the values of the constant (α) used in both gravity models is 2, it is possible to estimate the distribution of population and service employment between these five zones.

The first step in the calculation is to estimate the values of the scaling factors A_i and B_j which are required for the gravity models presented in eqs (4.10) and (4.14). When estimated by the method described in the preceding section the following values are obtained for this case:

Zone	A_i (eq (4.15))	B_j (eq (4.11))
1	0·590	0·310
2	1·641	0·303
3	3·121	0·311
4	0·358	0·279
5	1·045	0·233

Given these values, the first iteration of the model begins with the distribution of the work trips to the 1000 basic jobs that are located in zone 1 by means of an attraction constrained gravity model (eq (4.10)). The results of this distribution which are shown in full in table 4.4, indicate that 776 of the 1000 workers in zone 1 would, under these circumstances, also live in zone 1. Only 37 would live in zone 2 and 17 in zone 3. When these estimates of resident workers are converted to estimates of resident population using eq (4.13) the number of people living in these zones will be 1939 (ie, $776 \times 1/0·40$), 93 (ie, $37 \times 1/0·40$), and 42 (ie, $17 \times 1/0·40$) respectively.

The distribution of resident population can now be used to estimate the distribution of service employment using a production constrained gravity model (eq (4.14)) to generate the distribution of service trips made by them. Table 4.4 shows that 1430 of the 1939 residents of zone 1 obtained their services locally within the zone and most of the remainder travelled to zone 4 for this purpose. Apart from the residents of zone 5 who were divided relatively evenly between local services and the services provided by zone 4, most residents obtained their services locally within their zone of residence.

When summed up the service trips distributed to each zone can be converted to estimates of service employment by reference to the population service ratio. This shows that the resident population generated by the basic employment during this iteration has generated 500 service jobs of which 294 are located in zone 1 and 159 in zone 4.

These estimates of service employment can now be used to generate further estimates of resident population which will in turn give rise to additional numbers of service workers during the second iteration. The

TABLE 4.4

The Lowry model—worked example

FIRST ITERATION

Estimation of resident population (eqs (4.10), (4.12), (4.13))

		Employment					Resident	Resident
	Zone	1	2	3	4	5	workers	population
	1	776	0	0	0	0	776	1939
	2	37	0	0	0	0	37	93
Residence	3	17	0	0	0	0	17	42
	4	124	0	0	0	0	124	310
	5	47	0	0	0	0	47	116
Basic employment		1000	0	0	0	0	1000	2500

Estimation of service employment (eqs (4.14), (4.16), (4.17))

		Services					Resident
	Zone	1	2	3	4	5	population
	1	1430	23	5	458	23	1939
	2	8	76	2	7	1	93
Residence	3	3	3	32	3	0	42
	4	22	1	0	278	9	310
	5	6	1	0	49	61	116
Total service trips		1469	103	39	794	94	2500
Service employment		294	21	8	159	19	500

Second Iteration

Estimation of resident population (eqs (4.10), (4.12), (4.13))

	Zone	Employment					Resident workers	Resident population
		1	2	3	4	5		
	1	228	1	0	18	0	247	617
	2	11	19	0	2	0	33	81
Residence	3	5	1	7	1	0	14	36
	4	37	0	0	111	2	149	374
	5	14	0	0	27	16	57	142
Total employment		294	21	8	159	19	500	1250

Note: Numbers may not add up precisely because of rounding.

population generated in each of five iterations of this kind and the resulting overall distribution of population in the region is:

Iteration number:

Zone	1	2	3	4	$5 \times K$	Total
1	1939	617	226	94	85	2961
2	93	81	50	27	29	281
3	42	36	23	13	13	127
4	310	374	227	121	124	1156
5	116	142	99	57	61	475
Total	2500	1250	625	312·5	312·5	5000

(where K is the scaling factor required to balance the totals).

The numbers of service employees generated in each iteration and the overall distribution of service employment is:

Iteration number:

Zone	(basic)	1	2	3	4	$5 \times K$	Total
1	(1000)	294	100	39	17	16	466
2	(0)	21	16	9	5	5	56
3	(0)	8	6	4	2	2	22
4	(0)	159	109	61	32	32	392
5	(0)	19	19	12	7	7	64
Total	(1000)	500	250	125	62·5	62·5	1000

(where K is the scaling factor required to balance the totals).

The distribution of population and service employment that is predicted by this model generally illustrates the implications of the initial assumptions made about the relative accessibility and attractiveness of each zone. Over half of the total population is allocated to zone 1, mainly because the basic jobs are located in this zone, and the more accessible zones 4 and 5 account for the bulk of the remaining population. Service employment is shared mainly between zones 1 and 4 as a result of the values of the service trip attraction factors used for these zones and a consequence of the attraction of service trips to zone 4 is that an increasing proportion of the additional residential population and service employment is attracted to this zone and the neighbouring zone 5 in subsequent iterations of the model.

Models of this type together with more elaborate versions of the service employment and the residential location submodels can be used for a variety of purposes in urban and regional planning studies. Like the initial family of models, they can be used in impact analysis to evaluate the consequences of proposals which affect the attractiveness of one zone or set of zones in relation to the rest of the area, and they can also be used to examine the consequences of overall changes in personal behaviour in certain situations. In this case, examples of the former might include changes in basic employment, residential attractiveness, and service attractiveness in the Lowry model, and examples of the latter might include changes in either trip functions, activity rates or the population service ratio. The use of the model for these purposes can be illustrated by two simple examples with reference to the five-zone model described above. A possible topic for impact analysis might be an examination of the likely effects of a considerable increase in the amount of service floor space (and consequently service attraction) in zone 3 from 1000 to 5000 square feet, while the consequences of changes in personal behaviour might be explored by using 1 instead of 2 for the value of α in the work trip function.

Zone	Population distribution			Service employment distribution		
	Initial case	Impact analysis	Change in work trip function	Initial case	Impact analysis	Change in work trip function
1	2961	2940	1795	466	456	309
2	281	269	672	56	50	122
3	127	185	480	22	48	78
4	1156	1138	1120	392	384	381
5	475	468	933	64	62	110
Total	5000	5000	5000	1000	1000	1000

The results of these studies give some indication of how models of this type might respond to changed situations. The impact of the fivefold increase in floor space in zone 3 is reflected in a doubling of service employment in this zone and a fifty per cent increase in the residential population, but zone 3 remains, in spite of these increases, the smallest zone in terms of both residential population and service employment, and the relative strengths of the other zones are only marginally altered by this change. On the other hand a change in the work trip function can be seen to lead to dramatic repercussions throughout the area as a whole in terms of the distribution of both population and service employment. This change in work trip behaviour benefits those residential zones whose development was previously hampered by their relative isolation while the vast majority of the service trips remain as before to local centres. One consequence of this change in travel behaviour is that there is nearly fourfold increase in service employment in zone 3 where service floor space remained at 1, whereas an increase in the amount of service floor space in this zone to 5 previously stimulated only a doubling of its service employment.

3 *Statistical Formulation of the Gravity Model*

The family of gravity models provides a useful means of describing spatial inter-relationships even though their rationale is based solely on an analogy between the behaviour of urban and regional systems and the behaviour of physical systems. Recently, however, the work of Wilson and others (Wilson 1967, 1970a) has led to a statistical derivation of these models by means of an entropy maximising methodology which enables a more satisfactory theoretical interpretation to be given to their results. Like the concept of gravity, the concept of entropy is derived from physics where it is used in statistical mechanics to explain the properties of a system as a whole without having to explain the behaviour of each component of the system. When applied to trip distribution models this concept can be used to predict the overall distribution of trips within the system under consideration without having to explain the behaviour of each trip maker.

In statistical terms the concept of entropy is closely related to the level of uncertainty that exists about possible states of the system. Entropy is maximised when a state of the system as a whole is identified which expresses the largest number of possible individual states in this system, given that there are no grounds for choosing between them. In this way, then, the concept can be seen in statistical terms as relating to a probability distribution which recognises the uncertainty that exists about individual behaviour.

As a result of using the entropy maximising methodology each member of the gravity model family must be reformulated to incorporate an additional cost constraint and the simple power function used to represent the effect of distance is replaced by a negative exponential function. Under these circumstances, then, the production and attraction constrained gravity model (eqs (4.3) to (4.5)) would become:

$$T_{ij} = A_i B_j O_i D_j \, e^{-\beta c_{ij}} \tag{4.18}$$

$$\text{where} \quad A_i = 1/\sum_j B_j D_j \, e^{-\beta c_{ij}} \tag{4.19}$$

$$B_j = 1/\sum_i A_i O_i \, e^{-\beta c_{ij}} \tag{4.20}$$

and there are three sets of constraints:

$$\sum_j T_{ij} = O_i$$

$$\sum_i T_{ij} = D_j$$

$$\sum_i \sum_j T_{ij} c_{ij} = C$$

In this case T_{ij} is the number of trips made by residents in zone i to work in zone j.

O_i is the number of workers living in zone i.

D_j is the number of jobs in zone j.

c_{ij} is the cost of travelling between zone i and zone j.

β is a constant.

C is the total expenditure on travel to work.

e is the exponential number.

The main change in the reformulated model is that the effect of distance on interaction is expressed in terms of costs of travel between zones which must be related to the overall cost of travel by means of the new constraint. In addition to balancing productions and attractions, then, the distribution that is predicted by the model must also satisfy this additional cost constraint and represents as a result the most probable distribution of trips that will result from a predetermined cost of travel in the system as a whole.

Similar changes must also be made in the production constrained and the attraction constrained versions of the gravity model to meet the requirements of the entropy maximising methodology. The solution of these models is carried out by the same means as before, but the additional cost constraint (C) must be obtained, like the estimates of productions and/or attractions, from external sources. In this case, of course, a set of mathematical tables is required to calculate the values of the exponential functions. For instance, the value of $e^{-\beta c_{ij}}$ where the cost of travel (c_{ij}) is 10 units and β is 0·2 would be 0·1353 (ie, $1/\exp(0·2 \times 10) = 1/\exp 2 = 1/7·389$).

4 General Principles Governing the use of Interaction Models in Planning Studies

Both in their initial form and in their entropy maximising derivation the family of interaction models has a wide range of applications in urban and regional planning as an analytical tool and as a means for exploring the implications of changes in distribution and changes in behaviour. However, certain general considerations should be borne in mind when contemplating the development of operational models. Firstly, it should be noted that the gravity model is fundamentally a static model in the sense that it is only capable of describing interaction at one point in time. As a result it largely ignores the processes of locational and behavioural change that have created the interaction at that point in time, or otherwise treats them implicitly within the estimation procedures. For the same reason models of this kind can give only limited insight into the future even when they are used in relation to conditional predictions of the kind illustrated above that indicate what would happen if certain key variables were changed in a specified way.

Secondly, the single constraint versions of the model also make implicit assumptions about the equilibrium that is achieved when demand balances supply which is rarely found in real life situations.

The production constrained model, for instance, is a demand model which gives some indication of the potential demand for the attraction facilities. Whether facilities are supplied to meet this demand or not depends on a number of additional factors which are not directly included in the model. In the case of the retail location model it is common to find in operational situations cases where, for historical reasons, a relatively large number of outlets are competing for a declining demand in the inner areas of a city while a limited number of outlets are able to take advantage of a growing demand in the outer suburbs.

An additional cause of disequilibrium may be the wide range of possible institutional, physical, planning, and other constraints that are imposed on certain districts. In the attraction constrained residential location model, the development of a district for housing purposes may be inhibited by its lack of drainage facilities or simply by the unwillingness of a landowner to sell his property, even when its potential for housing appears to be considerable. In this case, as in that of the retail location model, then, additional constraints must be introduced into the operational model to ensure that it takes account of these factors. Generally speaking, however, the extent of these problems will be largely a function of the speed at which the sector which is modelled adjusts towards equilibrium in the real world. In retail trade where adjustment towards equilibrium is relatively rapid far fewer difficulties should be encountered than in residential location models where the process of adjustment takes place over a much longer period of time.

In addition to these considerations certain extra assumptions must be made in operational gravity models. Implicitly or explicitly, these must deal with the question of leakages in the sense that the interaction between the area under consideration and other regions or urban areas must be specified. In journey-to-work models leakages may be a relatively minor issue concerning a small number of workers who travel to work across the boundaries of the study area, but in retail location models account must be taken of occasional expenditures in the area by visitors and local residents' expenditure outside the area not merely as a

result of trips to other centres but also mail order purchases and indirec
buying.

A number of simplifying assumptions must also be made about th
spatial relationships in the model which may affect the validity of it
results. The individual units of behaviour must be grouped into spatia
units or zones according to certain criteria. Then a central point o
centroid must be located within each zone to act as the starting poin
for all the trips that are made from this zone, and some method must b
devised to estimate the distances or the costs of travel between eacl
zone centroid. In the case of trips within a zone this calculation ma
present considerable difficulties in its own right.

Apart from these considerations, most of the interaction models tha
can be used to estimate the distribution of population and economi
activities in regions and urban areas embody a number of additiona
assumptions about behaviour. The Lowry model, for instance, incor
porates a version of the export base multiplier whose limitations hav
already been discussed in the preceding section. It also assumes tha
residential locational preferences are related to individuals rather tha
groups of individuals living together as households. These consideration
as well as those relating to the use of gravity models should be borne i
mind when contemplating the development of models of this kind fo
planning purposes.

Further Reading

Most textbooks on urban analysis treat the subject largely in descrip
tive terms from a land use or ecological viewpoint which is of limitec
value in respect of studies of spatial organisation, but McLoughlin
(1969, pp 125–165) contains a useful chapter which sets out the genera
framework for a more systematic study. His approach is strongl
influenced by the work of Chapin and his associates on activity system
(Chapin, 1965a, pp 221–253 and Chapin and Hightower, 1966) and b
the communications theories of urban growth put forward by Meie
(1962) and Webber (1963 and 1964).

Three valuable review papers by Harris (1968a), Lowry (1968), and Wilson (1968) contain a more detailed discussion of spatial organisation in relation to the analytical models that have been developed for empirical work. Lowry's paper also contains an excellent summary of the processes represented in the urban land market, while Wilson's paper includes an extensive list of references. The economic theory underlying spatial organisation is derived from classical location and rent theory. It is represented largely by the work of Wingo (1961) and Alonso (1964) who have reformulated classical theory in terms of rent and transport costs in urban areas, although Muth (1969) has also made a valuable contribution to the study of price systems in urban housing markets.

The systematic study of travel behaviour in terms of producers and attractors dates back to Mitchell and Rapkin's (1954) study of Philadelphia and land use transportation studies such as the Chicago Area Transportation Study (1959) which have been reviewed by Oi and Shuldiner (1962). Most of these studies are concerned with traffic flows in large urban areas, although Taylor (1968)'s detailed analysis of three medium size English towns is an important exception to this general rule. By comparison with the transportation literature there is a dearth of general material on the spatial aspects of shopping expenditure and inter-industry linkages.

The family of gravity models is described by Cordey Hayes and Wilson (1971) in a paper which also reviews their statistical formulation and the derivation of an intervening opportunities model. An earlier review by Wilson (1970b) also discusses these models in terms of trip distribution modelling. The procedures involved in developing inter-action models for this purpose are described in relation to practical work in a manual prepared by the Bureau of Public Roads (1965). The general structure of the intervening opportunities model is explained in papers by Schneider (1959) and Harris (1964).

A basic reference for the Lowry model is the original work itself (Lowry, 1964), but considerable modifications have been made in subsequent work on this model. Reviews of this work which also discuss the range of applications to planning studies have been prepared by

Batty (1972), Goldner (1971), and Masser (1971). A detailed account of the procedures involved in the development of a version of this model for an operational planning situation has been prepared by the Centre for Environmental Studies as a result of their experience in conjunction with Cheshire County Planning Office (Barras *et al*, 1971).

The mathematical proof for the statistical derivation of the gravity model is explained fully in the work of Wilson ((1967) and (1970a, pp 1–14)). Readers with elementary mathematics may find this explanation difficult and are advised to begin with the other references by this author that are cited above, before they examine the mathematical proof of the model.

The main use of interaction models outside the analysis of travel behaviour has been in shopping studies. The development of shopping models is reviewed by Cordey Hayes (1968) and also by a committee of the National Economic Development Office (1970). Both of these contain useful lists of references and a discussion of the main applications of shopping models to planning studies.

The general review papers by Harris (1968a), Lowry (1968), and Wilson (1968) also describe a number of alternatives to interaction models which have been used in certain situations. These include the Chapel Hill model (Chapin, 1965b) which is concerned essentially with the processes underlying the conversion of land from agricultural to residential use, the Empiric model (Hill, 1965) which uses econometric techniques to estimate the changes that will occur in the zonal allocation of population and economic activities over a given period of time, the Herbert Stevens model (Herbert and Stevens, 1960) which involves the use of linear programming techniques to examine the structure of the market for residential land, and the San Francisco model (Little, 1966, pp 191–202) which simulates in considerable detail the factors affecting the supply of housing accommodation over time.

Apart from the models reviewed in these papers, an interesting model has been developed by Forrester (1969) to examine the life cycle of an urban area over a 250 year period. Unlike the models listed above, Forrester's model is essentially a theoretical model which is designed principally to examine the dynamics of urban growth and the effect of urban management programmes on these processes. His theoretical city is not presented in spatial terms, but in terms of interacting industries, housing units, and people. Nevertheless it points to some interesting avenues for the future development of spatial distribution models.

5. Towards Operational Models

Given a sound grasp of the basic methods that are available to analyse the growth of population and economic activity and their distribution within regions and urban areas it is possible to begin considering ways in which operational models are developed for particular purposes by planning agencies. The detailed consideration of these questions lies outside the scope of this book but, nevertheless, it is worth while concluding with a brief discussion of some basic considerations which must be taken into account when the methods that have been described in earlier chapters are embodied in operational models.

Two types of question should be borne in mind when considering the use of models in operational situations: firstly, the appropriate type of modelling techniques for the exercise in question, and secondly, the extent to which local circumstances and the technical resources that are available will influence the modelling effort. These can be conveniently labelled objectives and resources and discussed separately below.

Objectives

In any operational model it is essential that the objectives of the exercise are defined clearly at the start. In many cases, the precis definition of objectives is one of the most difficult parts of the modelling effort for it also presupposes an assessment of the appropriateness of available techniques in relation to the achievement of these objectives. Nevertheless it is crucial to all model building for as Lowry has noted,

> in communicating with an industrious but simple minded computer, all questions must be meticulously framed. In the process, false issues are unmercifully exposed, and others assume hitherto unsuspected importance. In the development of public policy, as in scientific research, the proper formulation of a question is the most important step in reaching an effective answer. (quoted in Loewenstein, 1966, pp 118–19)

Where there is a distinction between those involved in the construction of the model and those who frame the questions or use its output, communication problems may arise in connection with question formulation and the interpretation of output. In either case, those concerned should have sufficient understanding of the basic methods and assumptions underlying the operational model to be able to formulate questions and evaluate output with these considerations in mind. As the development of a model for any given situation will involve a host of detailed assumptions and simplifications, those involved in the construction effort must also bear the responsibility for presenting their work in such a way that these are made clear to interested parties. If they fail in this task there is a danger that the results of the exercise will be misused or misinterpreted even in situations where the initial questions have been formulated clearly.

This kind of situation is likely to occur particularly when the agencies responsible for model development are distinct from those concerned with its specification and its results. Consequently it is not surprising to find that one of the main reasons given to Hemmens during his survey of the modelling efforts of 26 American planning agencies to justify their preference for in-house projects as against using consultants or other external agencies in their work was 'the difficulty of generating adequate staff understanding of models produced outside the agency' (Hemmens 1968, p 223). Similar problems may also arise within planning agencies because of problems of communication between those in-

J

volved in the modelling effort and the rest of the agency staff. In the long term, operational models are likely to be used most effectively in situations where they reflect the basic philosophy and objectives of agency staff at all levels in the organisation.

Resources

Local circumstances, in terms of the kind of information that is available about the issue under consideration, the range and depth of previous analyses, and the technical resources that can be placed at the disposal of those involved in the modelling effort, should exert a profound influence on the type of model that is developed in any operational situation. Under these conditions a distinction must be made, as Alonso (1968) has pointed out, between errors that arise out of failings in the specification of the form and structure of the model that is to be used, and errors that occur because of inaccuracies in the information that forms the basis of the calculations performed within the model. Where the data that are available are relatively poor, errors resulting from inaccurate measurements are likely to be relatively high in an operational model by comparison with errors arising from its specification. In situations of this kind, which arise frequently in applied work, little is to be gained from sophisticated specifications of the model in question and simpler and more robust versions of the model are likely to produce equally effective results. Where errors of measurement are potentially high it may also be worth while developing several simple models which will explore related aspects of a single problem, rather than to concentrate on one elaborate model.

Alonso has proposed a set of rules that should be borne in mind in respect of the mathematical operations that are performed in these models. Since the effect of errors in measurement is accentuated wherever incremental values are used or variables are raised to a power he suggests that these operations should be avoided wherever possible in cases where the quality of the data is poor. In their place simple addition of values which results in the lowest cumulative error should be used as far as possible, and multiplication or division of values should be encouraged in preference to subtraction. Similarly, forms of model which proceed by chains in which each operation is dependent on a preceding operation or involve closely related variables should be avoided if possible.

The specification of models in operational circumstances should also take account of the range and depth of previous studies of the system and related topics which affect the exercise as a whole. Where there are few findings from previous studies to draw upon in the process of model development, the likelihood of error is increased even if the quality of the data used is relatively good because decisions affecting the structure of the model will have to be made in the absence of adequate information on the matter in question. Most of the models described above involve several kinds of aggregation in that individual decision making units are grouped to form aggregates whose behaviour is assumed to be homogeneous in themselves and distinct from other groups. Similar decisions must be made regarding the grouping of small areas into larger zonal units. If only partial and inadequate information from previous studies is available for this purpose, the increased possibilities of error that are likely to arise should be reflected in the model's specification. Alternatively resources should be diverted from the main modelling effort to remedy these deficiencies. Conversely, it may be possible to attempt relatively elaborate specifications for model development even in cases where this would otherwise not be justified by the quality of the information itself, as long as the experience of other studies can be drawn upon in the process.

Lastly, the technical resources that are available for each stage of the modelling effort should also be reflected in the form and specification of operational models. Apart from their development and calibration together with the interpretation and evaluation of their output, there are two other tasks which often make considerable demands on the technical resources that are available. Firstly, the collection and preparation of the information that is required for the model in its own right may absorb a high proportion of the available manpower particularly where sophisticated disaggregated models are envisaged. Secondly, especially in cases where large quantities of data are involved, a number of fundamental problems may have to be overcome in terms of the development of computing systems to make the model operational.

Before commencing a programme of model development a realistic appraisal should be made of the technical resources that are required in relation to those available for each stage of the exercise and the extent to which possible problems may arise which should be taken account of in the specification of the model. A striking feature of much past experience in this field has been the failure to appreciate the implications for technical resources of the specifications that were envisaged at the outset of many studies, and this has resulted in serious wastages of time and effort in the process of model development. Following a conference on Urban Development Models that was sponsored by the Highway Research Board in 1967, for instance, Britton Harris commented:

> One of the outstanding features of the somewhat impressionistic descriptions we have received of the process of model building is a confirmation of Thomas A. Edison's dictum that 'genius is two per cent inspiration and ninety-eight per cent perspiration'. In one case, for example, it was reported that the conceptualisation of a model took three days, and its implementation two years. The phenomenon of a flash of inspiration followed by considerable drudgery and hard work in making a model operational indeed seems to be the general case in many instances reported prior to the Conference (Harris, 1968b, pp 4–5).

Similarly, in their review of thirteen major land use transportation studies that were carried out in the United States in the first half of the 1960s, Boyce, Day, and McDonald found that,

> Considerable difficulties and delays were experienced in operationalising the theoretical models, and these were compounded by appreciable data management problems. Consequently, the number of alternatives prepared and the differences among them were severely limited and work schedules were drastically revised, often resulting in a loss of credibility for the planning effort (Boyce, Day, and McDonald, 1970, p 25).

Finally, it should be emphasised that the benefits arising out of the development of operational models in planning cannot be measured simply by reference to the extent to which their output results in decision taking. Operational models play an essential part in the continuous re-assessment of existing knowledge which leads to the definition of fresh lines for inquiry that is fundamental to the continued existence of the planning effort. The importance of this educational role in practical situations is stressed in Hemmens' (1968) survey of 24 American planning agencies which found that the dominant benefits experienced by these agencies as a result of the modelling effort was the education of planning agency staff. This resulted not only in a better knowledge of the nature of models but also a better understanding of local circumstances and a better understanding of the planning process itself through the clarification of basic concepts during the exercise of model development.

Appendix A

Matrix Operations—An Elementary Introduction to the Methods Used in the Text

Definition

A matrix is a rectangular array of numbers with m rows and n columns. The example below shows a matrix **B** with 2 rows and 3 columns:

$$\mathbf{B} = \begin{bmatrix} 4 & 5 & 6 \\ 2 & 1 & 2 \end{bmatrix}$$

A vector is a matrix with one row or one column. The examples below show vectors consisting of one row and three columns (**c**) and three rows and one column (**d**) respectively:

$$\mathbf{c} = \begin{bmatrix} 2 & 1 & 2 \end{bmatrix} \qquad \mathbf{d} = \begin{bmatrix} 4 \\ 5 \\ 6 \end{bmatrix}$$

The location of any element in a matrix or vector is given by the use of subscripts. Two subscripts are used for a matrix denoting the row number and the column number respectively. In matrix **B** above b_{12}

indicates the element in the first row and the second column of the matrix. In this case it would be 5. Similarly, b_{23} indicates the element in the second row and the third column of the matrix—that is 2. Only one subscript is required to locate an element of a vector. In vector **c** above c_2 would indicate the second element in the vector—that is 1, and d_3 in the vector **d** would indicate the third element of this vector, ie, 6.

Notation

Generally a standard form of notation is used to represent matrices, vectors, and the elements that they contain. In the rest of this section and throughout the sections of the book dealing with population and economic models, the following notation is used. The use of a capital letter in heavy type denotes a matrix while a subscripted lowercase letter is used to refer to an element of this matrix. A vector is referred to by the lowercase letter in heavy type and the elements of this vector by the subscripted lowercase letter.

$$\mathbf{B} = \begin{bmatrix} b_{11} & b_{12} & b_{13} \\ b_{21} & b_{22} & b_{23} \end{bmatrix}$$

$$\mathbf{c} = \begin{bmatrix} c_1 & c_2 & c_3 \end{bmatrix}$$

$$\mathbf{d} = \begin{bmatrix} d_1 \\ d_2 \\ d_3 \end{bmatrix}$$

Addition and Subtraction of Matrices

The sum of two matrices **A** and **B** is obtained by adding the corresponding elements of **A** and **B**:

$$\mathbf{A} = \begin{bmatrix} 3 & 5 & 8 \\ 4 & 1 & 0 \end{bmatrix} \qquad \mathbf{B} = \begin{bmatrix} 4 & 5 & 6 \\ 2 & 1 & 2 \end{bmatrix}$$

$$\mathbf{A}+\mathbf{B} = \begin{bmatrix} 3+4 = 7 & 5+5 = 10 & 8+6 = 14 \\ 4+2 = 6 & 1+1 = 2 & 0+2 = 2 \end{bmatrix} = \begin{bmatrix} 7 & 10 & 14 \\ 6 & 2 & 2 \end{bmatrix}$$

Similarly, the difference between two matrices **A** and **B** is obtained by subtracting the corresponding elements of **A** and **B**:

$$\mathbf{A-B} = \begin{bmatrix} 3-4= -1 & 5-5=0 & 8-6=2 \\ 4-2= 2 & 1-1=0 & 0-2=-2 \end{bmatrix} = \begin{bmatrix} -1 & 0 & 2 \\ 2 & 0 & -2 \end{bmatrix}$$

The necessary prerequisite for the addition or subtraction of matrices is that their dimensions be equal.

Multiplication of Matrices

Matrices can only be multiplied when the number of columns in the first matrix is equal to the number of rows in the second matrix. If this condition is satisfied, then, the product is a matrix **C** with the same number of rows as **A** and the same number of columns as **B**, whose element in the ith row and jth column is obtained by multiplying the elements of the ith row of **A** by the corresponding elements of the jth column of **B**, and summing up the products thus obtained. For instance:

$$\begin{bmatrix} 3 & 5 & 8 \\ 4 & 1 & 0 \end{bmatrix} \begin{bmatrix} 4 & 5 & 6 \\ 2 & 1 & 2 \end{bmatrix}$$

cannot be multiplied because the number of columns in **A** (3) does not equal the number of rows (2) in **B**. But,

$$\begin{bmatrix} 3 & 5 \\ 4 & 1 \end{bmatrix} \begin{bmatrix} 4 & 5 & 6 \\ 2 & 1 & 2 \end{bmatrix}$$

$$= \begin{bmatrix} (3\times4)+(5\times2)=22 & (3\times5)+(5\times1)=20 & (3\times6)+(5\times2)=28 \\ (4\times4)+(1\times2)=18 & (4\times5)+(1\times1)=21 & (4\times6)+(1\times2)=26 \end{bmatrix}$$

$$= \begin{bmatrix} 22 & 20 & 28 \\ 18 & 21 & 26 \end{bmatrix}$$

In this case c_{11} is calculated by multiplying the first row of **A** by the first column of **B**—ie,

$$c_{11} = a_{11}b_{11}+a_{12}b_{21} = (3\times4)+(5\times2) = 22$$

The same procedure is followed for the other elements until c_{23} is reached

$$c_{23} = a_{21}b_{13} + a_{22}b_{23} = (4 \times 6) + (1 \times 2) = 26$$

Multiplication of a matrix by a vector or a vector by a vector follows the same basic rules. For instance

$$\begin{bmatrix} 4 \\ 5 \\ 6 \end{bmatrix} \quad \begin{bmatrix} 2 \\ 1 \\ 2 \end{bmatrix}$$

cannot be multiplied, because the single column in **a** does not equal the three rows of **b**, but,

$$\begin{bmatrix} 4 \\ 5 \\ 6 \end{bmatrix} \begin{bmatrix} 2 & 1 & 2 \end{bmatrix} = \begin{bmatrix} 4 \times 2 = 8 & 4 \times 1 = 4 & 4 \times 2 = 8 \\ 5 \times 2 = 10 & 5 \times 1 = 5 & 5 \times 2 = 10 \\ 6 \times 2 = 12 & 6 \times 1 = 6 & 6 \times 2 = 12 \end{bmatrix}$$

$$= \begin{bmatrix} 8 & 4 & 8 \\ 10 & 5 & 10 \\ 12 & 6 & 12 \end{bmatrix}$$

Matrix multiplication does not necessarily satisfy the commutative law of mathematics whereby the product of $a \times b$ is always equal to the product of $b \times a$. In the case of the two vectors shown above, for instance, the product of $b \times a$ would be:

$$\begin{bmatrix} 2 & 1 & 2 \end{bmatrix} \begin{bmatrix} 4 \\ 5 \\ 6 \end{bmatrix} = [(2 \times 4) + (1 \times 5) + (2 \times 6) = 25] = [25]$$

Matrix Inversion

The inverse of a real number in ordinary arithmetic is another number so that their product is unity, ie, $ab = ba = 1$. A similar procedure can be followed for certain square matrices (ie, matrices where the number of rows is equal to the number of columns) so that $AB = BA = I$ (where I is the identity matrix).

In these cases the inverse matrix is found in the following way:

$$\mathbf{AB} = \mathbf{I}$$

where   **A** is the matrix $\begin{bmatrix} 3 & 5 \\ 3 & 6 \end{bmatrix}$

             B is the inverse matrix $\begin{bmatrix} b_{11} & b_{12} \\ b_{21} & b_{22} \end{bmatrix}$

             I is the identity matrix $\begin{bmatrix} 1 & 0 \\ 0 & 1 \end{bmatrix}$

If we apply **A** to **B** according to the matrix method of multiplication to obtain **I**, we arrive at two sets of two equations, each of which contains two unknown elements:

$$3b_{11} + 5b_{21} = 1 \qquad 3b_{12} + 5b_{22} = 0$$
$$3b_{11} + 6b_{21} = 0 \qquad 3b_{12} + 6b_{22} = 1$$

These can be solved as simultaneous equations, by solving the first equation in each set for one unknown:

$$b_{11} = (1 - 5b_{21})/3 \qquad b_{12} = -5b_{22}/3$$

and substituting the obtained value into the second equation in each set:

$$3(1 - 5b_{21})/3 + 6b_{21} = 0 \qquad 3(-5b_{22})/3 + 6b_{22} = 1$$

The solution of this system is:

$$b_{11} = 2 \qquad b_{12} = -\tfrac{5}{3}$$
$$b_{21} = -1 \qquad b_{22} = 1$$

Hence, the values of **B** can now be inserted in the equation **AB = I**.

$$\begin{bmatrix} 3 & 5 \\ 3 & 6 \end{bmatrix} \begin{bmatrix} 2 & -\tfrac{5}{3} \\ -1 & 1 \end{bmatrix} = \begin{bmatrix} (3 \times 2) + (5 \times -1) = 1 & (3 \times -\tfrac{5}{3}) + (5 \times 1) = 0 \\ (3 \times 2) + (6 \times -1) = 0 & (3 \times -\tfrac{5}{3}) + (6 \times 1) = 1 \end{bmatrix}$$

$$= \begin{bmatrix} 1 & 0 \\ 0 & 1 \end{bmatrix}$$

Similarly, $\mathbf{BA} = \mathbf{I}$ in this case,

$$\begin{bmatrix} 2 & -\frac{5}{3} \\ -1 & 1 \end{bmatrix} \begin{bmatrix} 3 & 5 \\ 3 & 6 \end{bmatrix}$$

$$= \begin{bmatrix} (2\times3)+(-\frac{5}{3}\times3) = 1 & (2\times5)+(-\frac{5}{3}\times6) = 0 \\ (-1\times3)+(1\times3) = 0 & (-1\times5)+(1\times6) = 1 \end{bmatrix}$$

$$= \begin{bmatrix} 1 & 0 \\ 0 & 1 \end{bmatrix}$$

Partitioning and Supermatrices

Matrices may be subdivided or partitioned to form submatrices. Similarly matrices may be combined to form supermatrices. The methods described above can be used in connection with either partitioned matrices or supermatrices as long as they satisfy the basic requirements of the calculations. As the elements of a supermatrix are in themselves matrices they are denoted by the use of capital letters, in heavy type, as in the case below of supermatrix $\mathbf{E}$:

$$\mathbf{E} = \begin{bmatrix} \mathbf{A} & 0 \\ 0 & \mathbf{B} \end{bmatrix}$$

where

$$\mathbf{A} = \begin{bmatrix} a_{11} & a_{12} \\ a_{21} & a_{22} \end{bmatrix}$$

$$\mathbf{B} = \begin{bmatrix} b_{11} & b_{12} \\ b_{21} & b_{22} \end{bmatrix}$$

Further Reading

The mechanics of the elementary matrix algebra used in the text are explained in this appendix without the mathematical proof of the methods. For further explanation of the mathematics involved and the general properties of matrices the reader is referred to the specialist literature.

Elementary introductions to matrix algebra with social science applications have been prepared by Horst (1963) and Peston (1967) and chapters dealing with this topic can also be found in most textbooks on mathematical economics or econometrics (eg, Chiang (1967) ch. 4 and 5, Johnston (1971) ch. 3). The mathematical processes themselves are treated in basic terms in Aitken (1964) and Lipschutz (1966), and in greater depth in the books by Hadley (1965) and Kemeny, Snell, and Thompson (1966).

Appendix B

Basic Computer Procedures for the Methods described in Chapters 2, 3, and 4

This appendix contains five Algol computer procedures which cover the methods described in Chapters 2, 3, and 4. These procedures carry out the mathematical operations described in the text and are written in such a way that they can be incorporated into simple computer programs which are suitable for most compilers once the local input and output requirements have been specified by the user. They are intended primarily to enable examples of the kind discussed in the text to be worked out and for small-scale applications to real situations.

The five procedures contained in this appendix are:

1   *Mult*
    Matrix formulation of the cohort survival model used in population projection (see Chapter 2).

2   *Inout*
    Matrix inversion for input–output analysis (see Chapter 3).

3 *Single term*

Solution of the production constrained gravity model used to estimate trip distribution and the sum of trip attractions (see Chapter 4).

4 *Double term*

Solution of the production and attraction constrained gravity model used to estimate trip distribution (see Chapter 4).

5 *Lowry*

Basic solution of the Lowry model used to estimate the distribution of population and service employment (see Chapter 4).

A standard format has been adopted in the presentation of each procedure which consists of the following elements:

1 The basic title of the procedure and specification of its formal parameters.

2 A comment statement describing its purpose and the specification of each variable.

3 The mathematical statements themselves, punctuated by comment statements describing their purpose.

4 Further notes on the specification and operation of the procedure.

1   Mult

```
procedure mult(m, n, pt, pt1, g) ;
integer m, n ;
array pt, pt1, g ;
comment this procedure multiplies an initial population matrix(pt)
containing m age groups and n regions by an m × m growth operator
(g) to estimate the values of the m × n population matrix(pt1) ;
begin integer i, j, k ;
  for i : = 1 step 1 until m do
  for j : = 1 step 1 until n do
  begin pt1 [i, j] : = 0 ;
          for k : = 1 step 1 until m do
          pt1 [i, j] : = pt1 [i, j] + g [i, k] × pt [k, j] ;
  end ;
end mult ;
```

Notes on Mult

1 General rules for operation:
In addition to the values of *g* and *pt* that are required for the calculations provision must also be made in the main body of the programme for *pt*1.

2 Inout

```
procedure inout(n, a, aa, b, g) ;
value n ;
integer n ;
array a, aa, b, g ;
comment this procedure estimates the n × n matrix of technical
coefficients(a) which express the inputs required to produce a unit
of output in the 1 × n gross output vector(g) for the n × n input
output table(aa) and calculates the n × n inverse matrix(b) which is
used to analyse the effects of a given change in final demand on
gross output ;

begin integer i, j, k, l, p ; real w, y ; array c, d [1 : n] ;
     integerarray z [1 : n] ;

              comment estimate the technical table(a) and the
              matrix to be inverted (b) ;
              for i := 1 step 1 until n do
              for j := 1 step 1 until n do
              begin a [i, j] := aa [i, j]/g [j] ;
                       if i = j then b [i, j] := 1 else b [i, j] := 0 ;
                       b [i, j] := b [i, j] - a [i, j] ;
              end ;

              comment invert(b) using Gauss Jordan elimination
              routine based on CACM 58 ;
              for j := 1 step 1 until n do z [j] := j ;
              for i := 1 step 1 until n do
              begin k := i ;
                       y := b [i, i] ;
                       l := i - 1 ;
                       p := i + 1 ;
                       for j := p step 1 until n do
                       begin w := b [i, j] ;
```

```
                        if abs(w) > abs(y) then
                        begin k := j;
                                y := w;
        end;      end;
        for j: = 1 step 1 until n do
        begin c[j] := b[j,k];
                b[j,k] := b[j,i];
                b[j,i] := − c[j]/y;
                d[j] := b[i,j] := b[i,j]/y;
            end;
            b[i,i] := 1/y;
            j := z[i];
            z[i] := z[k];
            z[k] := j;
            for k := 1 step 1 until l, p step 1 until n do
            for j := 1 step 1 until l, p step 1 until n do
            b[k,j] := b[k,j] − d[j] × c[k];
    end;
    l := 0;
    back: l := l+1;
    again: k := z[1];
    if k ≠ l then
    begin for i := 1 step 1 until n do
            begin w := b[l,i];
                    b[l,i] := b[k,i];
                    b[k,i] := w;
            end;
            z[l] := z[k];
            z[k] := k;
            goto again;
    end;
    if l ≠ n then goto back;
end inout;
```

Notes on Inout

1   The Gauss Jordan routine used in this procedure is based on an
    algorithm programmed by D. Cohen which was published in the
    Communications of the Association for Computing Machinery in
    May 1961 (CACM 58) and subsequently modified by R. Conger,
    R. George, and D. Struble.

2   General rules for operation:

   (a)   The sum of each row (ie, $\sum_j A_{ij}$) should be less than the gross output (G_i) for that row (unless final demand in that case equals 0).

   (b)   In addition to the values of aa and g that are required for the calculations provision must also be made in the main body of the program for a and b.

3   No provision is made in this procedure for cases where matrices are singular. If situations of this kind are expected a test should be made within the Gauss Jordan routine and provision made for exit to a non-local label in the main body of the program in these cases.

3   Single term

```
procedure singleterm(m, n, f, p, w, y, t, a, d) ;
value f ;
integer m, n ;
real f ;
array p, w, y, t, a, d ;
comment this procedure calculates the value of the balancing factor(a)
that is used in the production constrained gravity model and estimates
the resulting trip distribution(t) and the sum of attracted trips(d) for
m production zones and n attraction zones, given values for the 1 × m
vector of trip productions(p), the 1 × n vector of attraction factors for
the attraction zones(w), the m × n matrix of cost distances between
zones(y) and the distance function(f) ;
begin integer i, j ; real sl ;

        real procedure slope ;
        slope : = 1/y [i, j]↑sl ;

        comment estimate the values of a ;
                sl : = f ;
        for i : = 1 step 1 until m do
        begin a [i] : = 0 ;
                for j : = 1 step 1 until n do
                a [i] : = a [i] + w [j] × slope ;
                a [i] : = 1/a [i] ;
        end ;
```

K

```
        comment the basic trip distribution can be calculated
          using the values of a;
        for j:=1 step 1 until n do
        d[j]:=0;
        for i:=1 step 1 until m do
        for j:=1 step 1 until n do
        begin t[i,j]:=a[i]×p[i]×w[j]×slope;
              d[j]:=d[j]+t[i,j];
        end;
end singleterm;
```

Notes on Single Term

1 This procedure can also be used for the attraction constrained gravity model. In this case P_i will refer to the attractors (normally D_j in this model) and W_j to the attraction factor (normally W_i in this model).

2 *Variations in the distance function*
A simple power function $(1/d_{ij}^{\alpha})$ is used in this procedure, but alternative forms of distance function can be used simply by amending only one statement in the real procedure slope. The negative exponential function $(\exp(-\beta cij))$ would be:

$$\text{slope:} = \exp[-sl \times y(i,j)].$$

3 General rules for operation:

(a) Normally the distance function used should not be greater than 3 in the case of a simple power function or 1 in the case of the negative exponential function.

(b) In addition to the values of p, w, y, and f required for the calculations provision must also be made in the main body of the program for a, d, and t.

4 Double term

```
procedure doubleterm(m, n, d, p, y, a, b, t, eps, f, failure);
value eps, f;
integer m, n;
real eps, f;
array p, y, d, a, b, t;
label failure;
```

comment this procedure estimates the values of the balancing factors (*a* and *b*) that are used in the production and attraction constrained version of the gravity model, and calculates the resulting trip distribution(*t*)for *m* production zones and *n* attraction zones, given values for the 1 ×*m* vector of trip productions(*p*), the 1 ×*n* vector of trip attractions(*d*), the *m*×*n* matrix of cost distances between zones(*y*), and the distance function(*f*). The level of refinement required in the estimated values can be controlled by varying the parameter *eps*, and provision is made for exit to the label failure in situations where the system does not converge. Provision is made in the procedure for the output of the values of the balancing factors (*a* and *b*) together with the *m* × *n* matrix of trip distributions(*t*) ;

```
begin integer i, j; real c1, k, k1, k2, sl;
     realprocedure slope;
        slope := 1/y [i, j]↑sl;

        comment insert an initial value of b;
        for j := 1 step 1 until n do
        b [j] := 1;
        sl := f;
        k2 := 1000000;

        comment estimate a;
iter: for i := 1 step 1 until m do
        begin a [i] := 0;
                for j := 1 step 1 until n do
                a [i] := a [i] + b [j] × d [j] × slope;
                a [i] := 1/a [i];
        end;
        k := -10;

        comment estimate b, check that the system is
        converging and that the differences between
        the values are greater than eps;
        for j := 1 step 1 until n do
        begin c1 := 0;
                for i := 1 step 1 until m do
                c1 := c1 + a [i] × p [i] × slope;
                c1 := 1/c1;
                k1 := abs(c1 − b [j]);
                if k1 > k then k := k1;
                b [j] := c1;
        end;
```

K*

```
        if k2 < k then goto failure ;
        k2 := k ;
        if k > eps then goto iter ;

        comment when the values of a and b have been
        estimated the basic trip distribution can be
        calculated ;
        for i := 1 step 1 until m do
        for j := 1 step 1 until n do
        t[i,j] := a[i] × b[j] × p[i] × d[j] × slope ;
end doubleterm ;
```

Notes on Double Term

1   Generally values of 10^{-2} (ie, 0·01) or 10^{-3} (ie, 0·001) should be adequate for *eps*. If very small values are used for *eps* the number of iterations required before convergence occurs will increase considerably.

2   *Variations in the distance function*
A simple power function $(1/d_{ij}^{\alpha})$ is used in this procedure, but alternative forms of distance function can be used simply by amending only one statement in the real procedure slope. The negative exponential function $(\exp(\beta cij))$ would be:

$$slope: = \exp[-sl \times y(i,j)].$$

3   General rules for operation:

(a)   The sum of the trip productions $(\sum P_i)$ must be equal to the sum of the attractions $(\sum D_j)$.

(b)   In addition to the values of *d, p, y, eps, f* required for the calculation provision must also be made in the main body of the program for *a, b,* and *t,* and a label failure must also be inserted for cases of non-convergence.

5   Lowry

procedure lowry($m, z, dd, w, ww, y, tot1, tot2, tot3, tot4, f, ff, g, gg$) ;
value f, ff, g, gg, z ;
integer m, z ;
real f, ff, g, gg ;
array $y, dd, w, ww, tot1, tot2, tot3, tot4$;
comment this procedure carries out the basic operations of the lowry model in z iterations for a region consisting of m zones. It requires information for the following $1 \times m$ vectors, basic employment location (dd), residential attractiveness(w), service attractiveness (ww), an $m \times m$ cost distance matrix(y), a work trip function(f), a service trip function(ff), an activity rate(g) and a population service ratio(gg). Provision is made in the procedure for the output of predicted population($tot1$) predicted employment($tot2$, basic + service) in $1 \times m$ vectors and for work trip distributions($tot3$) and service trip distributions($tot4$) in $m \times m$ matrices ;
begin integer x, i, j ; **real** cc, sl ; **array** $a, b, d, p(1:m), e(1:m, 1:m)$;
　　　realprocedure slope ;
　　　slope $:= 1/y[i,j]\uparrow sl$;

　　　comment estimate the balancing factors required for the two gravity sub models ;
　　　$sl := ff$;
　　　for $i := 1$ **step** 1 **until** m **do**
　　　begin $a[i] := 0$;
　　　　　　for $j := 1$ **step** 1 **until** m **do**
　　　　　　$a[i] := a[i] + ww[j] \times$ slope ;
　　　　　　$a[i] := 1/a[i]$;
　　　end ;

　　　$sl := f$;
　　　for $j := 1$ **step** 1 **until** m **do**
　　　begin $b[j] := 0$;
　　　　　　for $i := 1$ **step** 1 **until** m **do**
　　　　　　$b[j] := b[j] + w[i] \times$ slope ;
　　　　　　$b[j] := 1/b[j]$;
　　　end ;

　　　comment initialise stores and estimate the multiplier ;
　　　for $j := 1$ **step** 1 **until** m **do** $d[j] := dd[j]$;
　　　for $i := 1$ **step** 1 **until** m **do**
　　　begin $tot1[i] := 0$; $tot2[i] := 0$;

```
                for j:=1 step 1 until m do
                begin tot3[i,j]:=0;
                        tot4[i,j]:=0;
                end;
        end;
        cc:=g/(g-gg);

        comment start basic set of iterations;
        for x:=1 step 1 until z do
        begin for j:=1 step 1 until m do
                begin if x=z then d[j]:=d[j]×cc;
                        tot2[j]:=tot2[j]+d[j];
                end;
                comment estimate work trip distribution and
                residential location;
                sl:=f;
                for i:=1 step 1 until m do
                begin p[i]:=0;
                        for j:=1 step 1 until m do
                        begin e[i,j]:=b[j]×d[j]×w[i]×slope;
                                tot3[i,j]:=tot3[i,j]+e[i,j];
                                p[i]:=p[i]+e[i,j];
                        end;
                        p[i]:=p[i]/g;
                        tot1[i]:=tot1[i]+p[i];
                end;

                comment estimate service trips and service
                employment;
                sl:=ff;
                for i:=1 step 1 until m do
                for j:=1 step 1 until m do
                begin e[i,j]:=a[i]×p[i]×ww[j]×slope;
                        tot4[i,j]:=tot4[i,j]+e[i,j];
                end;
                for j:=1 step 1 until m do
                begin d[j]:=0;
                        for i:=1 step 1 until m do
                        d[j]:=d[j]+e[i,j]×gg;
                end;
        end;
end lowry;
```

Notes on Lowry

1 No record is kept of the values of population or service employment that are generated for each iteration. These can be obtained by inserting output statements at relevant points in the procedure.

2 *Variations in the distance function*

A simple power function $(1/d_{ij}^a)$ is used in this procedure, but alternative forms of distance function can be used simply by amending only one statement in the real procedure slope. The negative exponential function $(\exp(\beta c i j))$ would be:

$$\text{slope:} = \exp[-sl \times y(i,j)].$$

3 General rules for operation:

(a) The number of iterations (z) generally should be about 5.

(b) The population service ratio (gg) must not be greater than the activity rate (g).

(c) Normally the distance functions used should not be greater than 3 in the case of the simple power function or 1 in the case of the negative exponential function.

(d) In addition to the values of *dd*, *w*, *ww*, *y*, *f*, *ff*, *g*, and *gg* that are required for the calculations provision must also be made in the main body of the program for tot 1, tot 2 and tot 3 and tot 4.

Bibliography

Aitken, A.C. (1964). *Determinants and matrices*, 9th edition, London.

Alonso, W. (1964). *Location and land use*: toward a general theory of urban rent, Cambridge, Mass.

Alonso, W. (1968). The quality of data and the choice and design of predictive models in Hemmens, G. C. (ed.) *Urban development models*. Highway Research Board Special Report 97, Washington DC.

Barras, R., Broadbent, T. A., Cordey Hayes M., Massey, D. B., Robinson, K., and Willis, J. (1971). An operational urban development model of Cheshire. *Environment and Planning* **3**, 115–234.

Batty M. (1972). Recent developments in land use modelling: a review of British research. *Urban Studies* **9**, 155–177.

Benjamin, B. (1968). *Demographic analysis*, London.

Beshers, J. M. (1967). *Population processes in social systems*, New York.

Bolan, R. S. (1967). Emerging views of planning. *Jour A.I.P.* **33**, 233–245.

Boudeville, J. R. (1966). *Problems of regional economic planning*, Edinburgh, Scotland.

Boyce, D., Day, N., McDonald, C. (1970). *Metropolitan plan making*. Regional Science Research Institute Monograph Series 4, Philadelphia.

Bruton, M. J. (1970). *Introduction to transportation planning*, London.

Bureau of Public Roads (1965). *Calibrating and testing a gravity model for any size urban area*, Washington, DC.

Bureau of the Census (1966). *Methods of population estimation*: Part I Illustrative procedure of the Census Bureau's component method II. Current Population Reports Series p. 25 no. 339.

Central Statistical Office (1970). *Input output tables for the United Kingdom 1963*. Studies in official statistics No. 16, London.

Chadwick, G. F. (1971). *A systems view of planning*: toward a theory of the urban and regional planning process, London.

Chapin, F. S. (1965a). *Urban land use planning*, 2nd Ed., Urbana, Ill.

Chapin, F. S. (1965b). A model for simulating residential development. *Jour A.I.P* **31**, 120–125.

Chapin, F. S. and Hightower, H. C. (1966). *Household activity systems*—a pilot investigation, Chapel Hill, NC.

152

Chiang, A. C. (1967). *Fundamental methods of mathematical economics*, New York.

Chicago Area Transportation Study (1959). *Final Report* Vol. I Survey Findings; Vol. II Data projections, Chicago Ill.

Cordey Hayes M. (1968). *Retail location models*. Centre for Environmental Studies, Working Paper 16, London.

Cordey Hayes M. and Wilson A. G. (1971). Spatial interaction. *Socio-Economic Planning Sciences* 5, 73–95.

Creighton, R. L. (1970). *Urban transportation planning*, Urbana, Ill.

Czamanski, S. (1969). Regional econometric models: a case study of Nova Scotia; in Scott, A. J. (ed.) *Studies in regional science*, London.

Duesenberry J., *et al.* (1965). *The Brookings Quarterly econometric model of the United States*, Amsterdam.

Edey, H. C., *et al.* (1967). *National income and social accounting*, 3rd edition, London.

Forrester, J. W. (1969). *Urban dynamics*, Cambridge, Mass.

Goldner, W. (1971). The Lowry model heritage. *Jour A.I.P.* 37, 100–110.

Hadley, G. (1965). *Linear algebra*, Reading, Mass.

Harris, B. (1960). Plan or projection: an examination of the use of models in planning. *Jour A.I.P.* 26, 265–272.

Harris, B. (1964). A note on the probability of interaction at a distance. *Journal of Regional Science* 5, 2, 31–35.

Harris, B. (1965). Urban development models—a gloss on lacklustre terms. *Jour A.I.P.* 31, 94–95.

Harris, B. (1966). The uses of theory in the simulation of urban phenomena. *Jour A.I.P.* 32, 258–273.

Harris, B. (1968a). Quantitative models of urban development: their role in metropolitan policy making; in Perloff, H. S. and Wingo, L. (eds.) *Issues in urban economics*, Baltimore, Md.

Harris, B. (1968b). Conference summary and recommendations; in Hemmens, G. C. (ed.) *Urban development models*, Highway Research Board Special Report 97, Washington, DC.

Hemmens, G. C. (1968). Survey of planning agency experience with urban development models, data processing and computers; in (ed.) *Urban development models*, Highway Research Board Special Report 97, Washington, DC.

Herbert, J. and Stevens, B. (1960). A model for the distribution of residential activities in urban areas. *Journal of Regional Science* 2, 21–36.

Hill, D. M. (1965). A growth allocation model for the Boston region. *Jour A.I.P.* 31, 111–120.

Horst, P. (1963). *Matrix algebra for social scientists*, New York.

Isard, W. (1960). *Methods of regional analysis*, an introduction to regional science, New York.

Johnston, J. (1971). *Econometric methods*, 2nd ed., New York.

Kemeny, J. G., Snell, J. L., and Thompson G. L. (1966). *Introduction to finite mathematics*, Engelwood Cliffs, NJ.

Keyfitz, N. (1964). Matrix multiplication as a technique of population analysis. *Millbank Memorial Fund Quarterly* 42, no. 3–4, 68–83.

Keyfitz, N. (1968). *An introduction to the mathematics of population*, Reading, Mass.

Klein, L. R. (1968). The specification of regional econometric models. *Papers and Proceedings RSA* **23**, 105–115.

Lane, T. (1966). The urban base multiplier: an evaluation of the state of the art. *Land Economics* **42**, 339–347.

Leven, C. L. (1961). Regional income and product accounts: construction and applications; in Hochwald W. (ed.) *Design of regional accounts*, Baltimore Md.

Lipschutz, S. (1966). *Theory and problems of finite mathematics*, New York.

Lipsey, R. G. (1971). *An introduction to positive economics*, 3rd ed, London.

Little, A. D. (1966). *Community Renewal Programming*: A San Francisco case study, New York.

Loewenstein, L. K. (1966). On the nature of analytical models. *Urban Studies* **3**, 112–119.

Lowry, I. S. (1964). *A model of metropolis*, Santa Monica, Cal.

Lowry, I. S. (1965). A short course in model design. *Jour A.I.P.* **31**, 158–166.

Lowry, I. S. (1968). Seven models of urban development: a structural comparison; in Hemmens, G. C. (ed.) *Urban development models*, Highway Research Board Special Report 97, Washington, DC.

McLoughlin, J. B. (1969). *Urban and regional planning*: a systems approach, London.

McLoughlin, J. B. and Webster, J. N. (1970). Cybernetic and general system approaches to urban and regional research: a review of the literature. *Environment and Planning* **2**, 369–408.

Masser, I. (1971). Possible applications of the Lowry model. *Planning Outlook* **11**, 46–59.

Masser, I., Coleman, A., and Wynn, R. F. (1971). Estimation of a growth allocation model for North West England. *Environment and Planning* **3**, 451–463.

Meier, R. L. (1962). *A communications theory of urban growth*, Cambridge, Mass.

Meyer, J. R. (1963). Regional economics—a survey. *American Economic Review* **53**, 19–54.

Miernyck, W. H. (1967). *The elements of input output analysis*, New York.

Ministry of Housing and Local Government (1970). *Projecting growth patterns within regions*. Statistics for town and country planning series III, population and households, Number 1, London.

Mitchell, R. B. and Rapkin, C. (1954). *Urban traffic, a function of land use*, New York.

Muth, R. F. (1969). *Cities and housing*: The spatial pattern of urban residential land use, Chicago.

National Economic Development Office (1970). *Urban models in shopping studies*. A report of the models working party of the Economic Development Committee for the Distributive Trades, London.

Oi, W. Y., and Shuldiner, P. W. (1962). *An analysis of urban travel demands*, Evanstown, Ill.

Olsson, G. (1965). *Distance and human interaction*: A review and bibliography. Regional Science Research Institute Bibliography Series No 2, Philadelphia, Pa.

Orcutt, G. H., Greenberger, M., Korbel, J., and Rivlin, A. M. (1961). *Microanalysis of socio economic systems*. A simulation study, New York.

Perloff, H. S., Dunn, E. S., Lampard, E. E., and Muth, R. F. (1960). *Regions, resources and economic growth*, Baltimore, Md.

Peston, M. (1967). *Elementary matrices for economists*, London.

Peterson, W. (1969). *Population*, Second edition, New York.

Pfouts, R. F. (1960). *The techniques of urban economic analysis*, New York.

Ridley, J. C. and Sheps, M. C. (1966). An analytic simulation model of human reproduction with demographic and biological components. *Population Studies* **19**, 297–310.

Rogers, A. (1966). Matrix methods of population analysis. *Jour. A.I.P.* **32**, 40–44.

Rogers, A. (1968). *Matrix analysis of interregional population growth and distribution*, Berkeley, Cal.

Samuelson, P. A. (1969). *Economics, an introductory analysis*, 8th ed, New York.

Schneider, M. (1959). Gravity models and trip distribution theory. *Papers and Proceedings RSA* **5**, 51–56.

Spiegelman, M. (1969). *Introduction to demography*, Revised edition, Cambridge, Mass.

Stone, R. and Croft Murray, G. (1959). *Social accounting and economic models*, London.

Stone, R. (1961). Social accounts at the regional level—a survey; in Isard, W. and Cumberland, J. H. (eds.) *Regional Economic Planning*, Paris.

Stone, R. and Brown, A. (1962). *A computable model of economic growth*. A programme for growth No. 1, Department of Applied Economics, University of Cambridge, Cambridge.

Taylor, M. A. (1968). Studies of travel in Gloucester, Northampton and Reading. *Road Research Laboratory Report LR141*, Crowthorne, Berks.

Thompson, E. J. (1968). Building a population model. *Quarterly Bulletin of the Research and Intelligence Unit* **2**, 25–29, Greater London Council, London.

Tiebout, C. M. (1962). *The community economic base study*. Committee for Economic Development Supplementary Paper No. 16, New York.

Ulman, E. L. and Dacey, M. F. (1960). The minimum requirements approach to the urban economic base. *Papers and Proceedings RSA* **6**, 175–194.

United Nations (1956). *Methods for population projections by sex and age*. Manuals on methods of estimating Population, Manual III, Sales No. 56 XIII, 3.

United Nations (1966). *Problems of input output analysis*. Studies in methods, Series F, No. 14. Sales No. 66 XVIII, 8, New York.

Webber, M. (1959). Preface to special issue on 'land use and traffic models—a progress report'. *Jour. A.I.P.* **25**, 55.

Webber, M. (1963). Order in diversity: community without propinquity; in Wingo, L. (ed.) *Cities and Space*, Baltimore, Md.

Webber, M. (1964). The urban place and the non place urban realm; in Webber M. *et al. Explorations into urban structure*, Philadelphia, Pa.

Webber, M. (1968). Planning in an environment of change I. Beyond the industrial age. *Town Planning Review* **39**, 179–195.

Webber, M. (1969). Planning in an environment of change II. Permissive planning. *Town Planning Review* **39**, 277–295.

Welch, R. L. (1971). *Migration in Britain*: data sources and estimation techniques. Occasional Paper 18, Centre for Urban and Regional Studies, University of Birmingham, Birmingham.

Willis, J. (1968). *Population growth and movement*. Centre for Environmental Studies Working Paper 12, London.

Wilson, A. G. (1967). A statistical theory of spatial distribution models. *Transportation Research* 1, 253–269.

Wilson, A. G. (1968). Models in urban planning: a synoptic review of recent literature. *Urban Studies* 5, 249–276.

Wilson, A. G. (1970a). *Entropy in urban and regional modelling*, London.

Wilson, A. G. (1970b). Advances and problems in distribution modelling. *Transportation Research* 4, 1–18.

Wingo, L. (1961). *Transportation and urban land*, Baltimore, Md.

Yan, C–S, (1969). *Introduction to input output economics*, New York.

Acknowledgements

The preparation of this book would have been impossible without the constant stimulus that comes from teaching, and I owe a great debt to classes of graduate students past and present and to my colleagues in the Department of Civic Design for their comments and suggestions which have found their way into the work. Although it is usually invidious to single out colleagues I must express my gratitude to Peter Brown for his help in checking material and computing procedures, and to Anne Dennier, Don Field, and Diane Macunovich for reading parts of the book in manuscript and for their helpful comments on the presentation of the material. I would also like to thank colleagues in other parts of Liverpool University who have made valuable comments during the preparation of the book, in particular Professor George Peters of the Department of Economics, Kathleen Pickett of the Department of Sociology and Grahame Settle of the Department oı Computational and Statistical Science. As always, however, none of these individuals is responsible for any errors or omissions in the work as these are part of the burden of authorship. Finally, as books of this kind present some formidable problems for the typist, sincere thanks are due to Clara Gay for her painstaking efforts in the preparation of the final manuscript.

My greatest debt is to my wife Alexandra for her constant encouragement during the frustratingly slow task of writing, and for her cheerful acceptance of the many sacrifices which go with writing a book. This volume is dedicated to her with respect and affection.

Index

159